First World War
and Army of Occupation
War Diary
France, Belgium and Germany

50 DIVISION
Divisional Troops
245 Machine Gun Company
15 July 1915 - 31 March 1918

WO95/2823/4

Published by

The Naval & Military Press Ltd

Unit 10 Ridgewood Industrial Park,

Uckfield, East Sussex,

TN22 5QE England

Tel: +44 (0) 1825 749494

www.naval-military-press.com

www.nmarchive.com

This diary has been reprinted in facsimile from the original. Any imperfections are inevitably reproduced and the quality may fall short of modern type and cartographic standards.

© Crown Copyright
Images reproduced by permission of The National Archives, London, England, 2015.

Contents

Document type	Place/Title	Date From	Date To
Heading	WO95/2823 50 Div 245 M.G.C. Jul 17-Mar 18		
Heading	50th Division No. 245 Machine Gun Coy. Jly 1917-1918 Mar		
Heading	War Diary of No. 245 Machine Gun Company. From 15th July 1917 To 31st August 1917 (Volume No. 1.)		
War Diary	Grantham	15/07/1915	15/07/1915
War Diary	Southampton	15/07/1915	15/07/1915
War Diary	Havre	16/07/1915	28/07/1915
War Diary	Fourcart Alvamare	29/07/1915	29/07/1915
War Diary	Romscamps Boisleux-au Mont	29/07/1915	29/07/1915
War Diary	Boisleux Au Mont	30/07/1915	30/07/1915
War Diary	Mercatel	31/07/1915	03/08/1915
War Diary	Mercatel & Trenches	04/08/1915	21/08/1915
War Diary	Mercatel Sheet 51B. (France) 1/40,000 M.24.C.2.4 & Trenches	22/08/1915	30/08/1915
Miscellaneous	Appendices.		
Map	Trench Map. Cherisy Sector. No. 6		
Operation(al) Order(s)	Appx No. 8 Operation Order No. 1 by Capt to WR Thomson Commdg 245 M.G. Coy.	12/08/1917	12/08/1917
Operation(al) Order(s)	245 M.G. Coy. Operation Order No. 2 Appendix No 11	19/08/1917	19/08/1917
Map	Appendix No. 12		
Operation(al) Order(s)	Operation Order No. 3. by Captain W.R. Thomson Commanding No 245 M.G. Coy. Appendix 14	28/08/1917	28/08/1917
Heading	War Diary of 245 Machine Gun Company From 1st Sept. 1917 To 30th Sept. 1917. (Volume 2)		
War Diary	Mercatel. Ref. O.S. France. Sheet 51B. M.24.C.2.4	03/09/1917	08/09/1917
War Diary	Carlisle Camp.	09/09/1917	30/09/1917
Miscellaneous	Appendices To War Diary of 245 Machine Gun Company From 1st Sept. to 30th Sept. 17	01/09/1917	01/09/1917
Operation(al) Order(s)	Operation Order No. 4 No. 245 M.G. Coy. Appendix 2.	05/09/1917	05/09/1917
Operation(al) Order(s)	Operation Order No. 5 by Capt W.R. Thomson Comdg 245 M.G. Coy. Appendix 6.	12/09/1917	12/09/1917
Map	Maps Showing Guns And Targets For Raid.		
Miscellaneous	Regt O.O. No. 5 Para 2 Appendix 7	15/09/1917	15/09/1917
Miscellaneous	German Official Sept 16th	16/09/1917	16/09/1917
Miscellaneous	30th. Division Intelligence Summary No. 102. From 12 Noon 15.9.17 to 12 Noon 16.9.17 Appendix 8	15/09/1917	15/09/1917
Operation(al) Order(s)	Operation Order No. 6 by Captn W.R. Thomson Commdg 245 M.G. Coy. Appendix 10.	21/09/1917	21/09/1917
Operation(al) Order(s)	Operation Order No. 7 by Captn W.R. Thomson Commanding 245 M.G. Coy. Appendix 14	27/09/1917	27/09/1917
Map	Map Showing M.G.S. In 50th Divl Sector Under VI Corps M.G. Defence Scheme.		
Heading	War Diary of No 245 Machine Gun Company From 1st Oct. To 31st Oct. 1917. Vol III		
Miscellaneous			
War Diary	Carlisle Camp Ref 51 B.S.W. 500 S. of Beaurains.	01/10/1917	04/10/1917
War Diary	Carlisle Camp	04/10/1917	05/10/1917
War Diary	Achiet-Le-Petit Lens II 1/100,000	05/10/1917	06/10/1917
War Diary	Achiet Le Petit	07/10/1917	17/10/1917

War Diary	Broxeele Ref 4 Hazebrouck 5A 1/100,000 Sheet 27	18/10/1918	21/10/1918
War Diary	La Cloche Refn Hazebrouck 5A 1/100,000	21/10/1917	21/10/1917
War Diary	La Cloche	22/10/1917	22/10/1917
War Diary	Proven (Refn. Hazebrouck 5A 1/100,000 & Sheet 27)	22/10/1917	24/10/1917
War Diary	Friedland Farm 28 N.W. 1/20,000 B.23.b.8.2	24/10/1917	27/10/1917
War Diary	Friedland Fm	27/10/1917	31/10/1917
Miscellaneous	List of Appendices To Accompany The War Diary.		
Miscellaneous	Appendix 2. OB/181	10/10/1917	10/10/1917
Operation(al) Order(s)	Operation Order No. 8 by Capt. W.R. Thomson Commanding 245 M.G. Coy.	03/10/1917	03/10/1917
Operation(al) Order(s)	Operation Order No. 9 by Capt. W.R. Thomson Commdg 245 M.G. Coy. Appx 4	04/10/1917	04/10/1917
Operation(al) Order(s)	Operation Order No. 10 by Capt. W.R. Thomson Commdg 245 M.G. Coy. Appx 6	15/10/1917	15/10/1917
Operation(al) Order(s)	Operation Order No.11 by Capt W R Thomson Commdg 245 M.G. Coy. Appx 9	21/10/1917	21/10/1917
Operation(al) Order(s)	Operation Order No 12 by Capt W R Thomson Commdg 245 M.G. Coy. Appx 11	21/10/1917	21/10/1917
Operation(al) Order(s)	Operation Order No 13 by Capt W R Thomson Commdg 245 M.G. Coy. Appx 13.	23/10/1917	23/10/1917
Operation(al) Order(s)	Operation Order No 14 by Capt W R Thomson Commdg 245 M.G. Coy. Appx 15	25/10/1917	25/10/1917
Operation(al) Order(s)	Appendix No 1 to Coy O.O. No. 14 Appx 15A	25/10/1917	25/10/1917
Heading	Map of Battle to accompany Coy. O.O. No. 15 and Coy O.O. No. 16 Appendix 14A		
Map	Appendix 14A to accompany Coy. O.O. No. (App.		
Heading	Map of Battle to accompany Coy. O.O. No. 15 and Coy. O.O. No. 16. Appendix 14A		
Operation(al) Order(s)	Operation Order No. 15 by Capt W R Thomson Commdg 245 M.G. Coy. Appx 17	27/10/1917	27/10/1917
Operation(al) Order(s)	Operation Order No. 16 by Capt W R Thomson Commdg 245 M.G. Coy. Appx 21	30/10/1917	30/10/1917
Heading	War Diary of 245 Machine Gun Company from 1st Nov. 1917 to 30th Nov. 1917 Volume IV		
War Diary	Friedland Farm B.23.b.8.2. Sheet 28.	01/11/1917	02/11/1917
War Diary	Sutton Camp F.10.b.6.5. Sheet 27	02/11/1917	10/11/1917
War Diary	Sutton Camp	10/11/1917	11/11/1917
War Diary	Hellebroucq Hazebrouck 5A 1/100,000 27A 1/20,000	12/10/1917	12/10/1917
War Diary	Hellebroucq	23/11/1917	23/11/1917
Miscellaneous	Appendices to War Diary of 245 M.G. Coy. for November 1917		
Operation(al) Order(s)	Operation Order No. 19 by Capt W R Thomson Commdg 245 M.G. Coy.	01/11/1917	01/11/1917
Operation(al) Order(s)	Operation Order No. 20 by Capt W R Thomson Commdg 245 M.G. Coy.	09/11/1917	09/11/1917
Operation(al) Order(s)	Addendum No. 1 to O.O. No. 20. by Capt. W R Thomson Commdg 245 M.G. Coy.	10/11/1917	10/11/1917
Heading	War Diary of No 245 Machine Gun Company From 1st December 1917 To 31st December 1917 (Volume V)		
War Diary	Hellebroucq (France 27A & Hazebrouck SA)	01/12/1917	10/12/1917
War Diary	Hellebroucq	10/12/1917	11/12/1917
War Diary	Ridge Camp Ref. 28 N.W. G.11.d.2.4	11/12/1917	12/12/1917
War Diary	No 3 HG Camp Potijze I.3.d.2.5 (28 N.W.)	13/12/1917	15/12/1917
War Diary	In The Line. Adv. Coy H.Q. Yne Cotts.	16/12/1917	17/12/1917
War Diary	In The Line Passchendaele Sector	18/12/1917	23/12/1917
War Diary	In The Line Passchendaele Sector. (Sheet 28 NE)	24/12/1917	31/12/1917

Type	Description	Date	Date
Operation(al) Order(s)	50th Division Order No. 148. Appx No. 1	07/12/1917	07/12/1917
Operation(al) Order(s)	Operation Order No. 24 by Capt W R Thomson Commdg 245 M.G. Coy.	09/12/1917	09/12/1917
Miscellaneous	Appx No. 4		
Map	Passchendaele Station		
Miscellaneous	Appx No. 4		
Miscellaneous	Appendix No. 1 to Coy O.O. No. 24	09/12/1917	09/12/1917
Miscellaneous	Organization of Machine Gun Companies In 50th Division. Appx No. 2 50th Division.	08/12/1917	08/12/1917
Operation(al) Order(s)	Operation Order No. 25 by Capt W R Thomson Commdg 245 M.G. Coy. Appx No. 3	11/12/1917	11/12/1917
Miscellaneous	Machine Gun Group 50th Division Operation Order No. 1 Appx No. 5	14/12/1917	14/12/1917
Miscellaneous	No. 245 M.G. Coy. O.O. No. 26 by Capt W.R. Thomson. Appx No. 6	15/12/1917	15/12/1917
Miscellaneous	Machine Gun Group 50th Division Operation Order No. 2 Appx 7	18/12/1917	18/12/1917
Operation(al) Order(s)	50th Division Operation Order No. 153 Appx No. 8	22/12/1917	22/12/1917
Miscellaneous	No 245 M.G. Coy O.O. 27 by Capt W.R. Thomson.	19/12/1917	19/12/1917
Miscellaneous	No 245 M.G. Coy O.O. 28 by Capt W.R. Thomson. Appx No. 9	22/12/1917	22/12/1917
Miscellaneous	Appendix No. 1. To 50th Division Provincional Defence Instructions. Machine Gun Defence.		
Miscellaneous	Machine Gun Defence Scheme. Appx No. 10		
Miscellaneous	Move of Surplus Personnel of 245 M.G. Coy. Appx No. 10A	26/12/1917	26/12/1917
Operation(al) Order(s)	50th Division Operation Order No. 155	26/12/1917	26/12/1917
Miscellaneous	No. 245 Machine Gun Coy. Operation Order No. 29 By Captain W.R. Thomson. Appx No. 11	26/12/1917	26/12/1917
Miscellaneous	245 M.G. Company. Appx. No. 11A		
Miscellaneous	50th Division Operation Order No. 156 Appx No. 12	30/12/1917	30/12/1917
Operation(al) Order(s)	Company Operation Order No. 30. Appx No. 13	31/12/1917	31/12/1917
Heading	War Diary of No. 245 Machine Gun Company From 1st January 1918 To 31st January 1918 (Volume VI.)		
War Diary	Potijze I.3.d.25	02/01/1918	05/01/1918
War Diary	Steenvoorde Q.1.C.1.Z. Sheet 27	10/01/1918	16/01/1918
War Diary	Westbecourt V 14.C. 20.90. Sheet 27 A.S.E.	24/01/1918	30/01/1918
War Diary	Potijze I.3.d.25	31/01/1918	31/01/1918
Operation(al) Order(s)	Machine Gun Group 50th Division Operation Order No. 1. Appx 1.		
Operation(al) Order(s)	50th Division Operation Order No. 159. Appx No. 2	09/01/1918	09/01/1918
Operation(al) Order(s)	245 Machine Gun Company Operation Order No. 32. Appx. No. 3	13/01/1918	13/01/1918
Operation(al) Order(s)	245 Machine Gun Company. After Order-Ref Operation Order No. 32 Appx No. 3	13/01/1918	13/01/1918
Operation(al) Order(s)	50th Division Operation Order No. 161 Appx No. 4	24/01/1918	24/01/1918
Miscellaneous	50th Division Operation Order No. 163 Appx No. 5	26/01/1918	26/01/1918
Operation(al) Order(s)	245th Machine Gun Company. Operation Order No. 33 Appx No. 6	27/01/1918	27/01/1918
Operation(al) Order(s)	50th Division Operation Order No. 166 Appx No. 7	31/01/1918	31/01/1918
Heading	War Diary of No. 245 Machine Gun Company From February 1st 1918 To February 28th 1918 (Volume VII)		
War Diary	Potijze I.3.d.25.	04/02/1918	22/02/1918
War Diary	Acquin 22.A.4.7 Sheet 27A SE.	22/02/1918	22/02/1918
Operation(al) Order(s)	50th Division (Machine Gun) Order No. 169. Appx No. 1	03/02/1918	03/02/1918

Miscellaneous	Relief Orders By Captain J.R. Houghton. O.C. M.G. Group In The Line. Appx No. 2	03/02/1918	03/02/1918
Operation(al) Order(s)	50th Division (Machine Gun) Order No. 170. Appx No. 2	03/02/1918	03/02/1918
Operation(al) Order(s)	50th Division (Machine Gun) Order No. 171. Appx No. 4	06/02/1918	06/02/1918
Operation(al) Order(s)	Company Operation Order No. 35. By Captain J.R. Houghton Commanding 245 M.G. Coy. Appx No. 5	06/02/1918	06/02/1918
Operation(al) Order(s)	50th Division (Machine Gun) Order No. 173. Appx No. 6	11/02/1918	11/02/1918
Operation(al) Order(s)	Operation Orders No. 36. Captain J.R. Houghton. Commanding 245th Machine Gun Company. Appx No. 7	11/02/1918	11/02/1918
Operation(al) Order(s)	50th Division (Machine Gun) Order No. 176. Appx. No. 8	15/02/1918	15/02/1918
Operation(al) Order(s)	Operation Order No. 37. Issued By Captain. J.R. Houghton. Commanding 245 Machine Gun Company. Appx No. 9	15/02/1918	15/02/1918
Operation(al) Order(s)	50th Division (Machine Gun) Order No. 178. Appx No. 10	17/02/1918	17/02/1918
Heading	50th Divisional Troops Became "D" Company 50th Machine Gun Battalion 245th Machine Gun Company March 1918		
Heading	War Diary of D Coy for March 1918		
War Diary	Acquin 22A. 4.7. Sheet 27A SE.	01/03/1918	08/03/1918
War Diary	Blangy-Tronville	10/03/1918	10/03/1918
War Diary	Sheet 17. Amiens	11/03/1918	11/03/1918
War Diary	Vauvillers Sheet 17 Amiens	12/03/1918	20/03/1918
War Diary	Vauvillers (Ref Amiens 17)	21/03/1918	21/03/1918
War Diary	Ref. Sheet 62 C 1/40,000 & St. Quentin Sheet 18 1/100,000 Beaumetz	22/03/1918	22/03/1918
War Diary	Beaumetz St. Cren	23/03/1918	23/03/1918
War Diary	Brie Ref 62 C 1/40,000 & Amiens 17 1/100,000.	23/03/1918	23/03/1918
War Diary	Ref 62C N.33.b.	23/03/1918	23/03/1918
War Diary	Chaulnes	24/03/1918	24/03/1918
War Diary	Foucaucourt	24/03/1918	24/03/1918
War Diary	Foucaucourt (62.C 1/40,000 & Amiens 17)	25/03/1918	26/03/1918
War Diary	Vauvillers	26/03/1918	26/03/1918
War Diary	Harbonnieres	27/03/1918	28/03/1918
War Diary	Caix	28/03/1918	28/03/1918
War Diary	Caix (Amiens 17 1/100,000)	28/03/1918	28/03/1918
War Diary	Ignaucourt	28/03/1918	28/03/1918
War Diary	Demuin	29/03/1918	29/03/1918
War Diary	Domart	29/03/1918	29/03/1918
War Diary	Domart (Amiens 17)	29/03/1918	29/03/1918
War Diary	Boves	30/03/1918	30/03/1918
War Diary	Sains-En-Amienois	30/03/1918	31/03/1918
Operation(al) Order(s)	149th Infantry Brigade Warning Order No. 243 Appx No. 1	28/02/1918	28/02/1918
Operation(al) Order(s)	149th Infantry Brigade Operation Order No. 244. Appx No. 2	08/03/1918	08/03/1918
Operation(al) Order(s)	Operation Order No. 37 By Captain W.R. Thomson Commanding 245 Machine Gun Coy. Appx No. 3	08/03/1918	08/03/1918
Operation(al) Order(s)	Operation Order No. 38. By Captain W.R. Thomson Commanding 245 Machine Gun Coy. Appx 4	10/03/1918	10/03/1918

Type	Description	Date	Date
Operation(al) Order(s)	Warning Order No. 39 by Capt. W.R. Thomson Commanding 245 M.G. Coy. Appx 5	12/03/1918	12/03/1918
Operation(al) Order(s)	Warning Order No. 40 by Capt. W.R. Thomson Commanding 245 M.G. Coy. Appx 6	13/03/1918	13/03/1918
Miscellaneous	Ref. Sheet 57C S.E. 1/20,000 Appx 7		
Miscellaneous			
Map	Map No. 1		
Miscellaneous	Appendix 8. Copies of Telegrams Received From M.G. Battn.		
Map	Appendix 9. St. Quentin		
Map	Parts of Skt. Amiens & St. Quentin.		
Map			
Diagram etc	Appx 11		
Diagram etc	Appx 12		
Operation(al) Order(s)	Operation Order No. 41 by Capt W R Thomson Commdg 245 M.G. Coy. Appx 13	30/03/1918	30/03/1918
Miscellaneous	XIX Corps Administrative Instructions No. 98 Appx 14	30/03/1918	30/03/1918
Operation(al) Order(s)	Coy. By Warning Order No. 42 by Capt W R Thomson Commdg 245 M.G. Coy. Appx 15	31/03/1918	31/03/1918

WO95/2823
50 Div
245 M.G.C.
Jul '17 – Mar '18

(4)

50TH DIVISION

NO. 245 MACHINE GUN COY.

JLY 1917-APR 1919

1918 MAR

CONFIDENTIAL

WAR DIARY

OF

No 245 MACHINE GUN COMPANY.

FROM 15th JULY 1917 TO 31st AUGUST 1917.

(VOLUME I No 1.)

Army Form C. 2118.

WAR DIARY
or
INTELLIGENCE SUMMARY.
(Erase heading not required.)

Instructions regarding War Diaries and Intelligence Summaries are contained in F. S. Regs., Part II. and the Staff Manual respectively. Title pages will be prepared in manuscript.

Place	Date	Hour	Summary of Events and Information	Remarks and references to Appendices
GRANTHAM	JULY 15°	2·25 A.M.	Left by train for Southampton. 10 officers 177 other Ranks.	
SOUTHAMPTON	15°	5·30 P.M.	Embarked and sailed for Havre in H.M.T. "AUSTRALIND"	
HAVRE	16°	8·30 A.M.	Disembarked and marched to N°1 Rest Camp. Sect" A at SANVIC. A.S.C. driver joined.	
"	17°		Making up deficiencies in equipment clothing transport M.G.'s &c.	
"	18°		do.	
"	19°		do.	
"	20°			
"	21st		In rest camp.	
"	22nd			
"	23rd		1 N.C.O. to Hospital, Sick.	
"	24°		1 O.R. to hospital sick	
"	25°		1 O.R. to hospital Sick.	
"	26°		1 NCO from hospital. 2 O.R. struck off strength returned above	
"	28th		Movement Orders received. Left Rest Camp 9·30 p.m. 1 Horse coat.	N° 1 Movement Order
"	29th	3·20 A.M.	Entrained and departed. Strength 10 offrs, 176 O.R., 6 Riders, 2 H.D., 47 mules.	Entrainment order DAQHG Base HAVRE
FOURCART-AIVAMARE	"	5·30 A.M.	Horse-truck broken during shunting; containing 6 Riders & 2 H.D. left behind in siding at FOURCART-AIVAMARE Stn in charge of Transport Sgt & 5 men. Arrangements made by French authorities to have another truck sent up from LE HAVRE.	
ROMESCAMPS	"	2 P.M.	Stopped for meal. Left ROMESCAMPS 9·45 p.m. via ALBERT & AMIENS	
BOISLEUX -au-Mont	30th	4·30 A.M.	Arrived. Met by Divl H.Q.O. Marched to Camp N.W. of MERCATEL. Reported to G.O.C. 150th I. Bde. Informed that the Bn is to be	

A5834 Wt. W4973/M687 750,000 8/16 D.D. & L. Ltd. Forms/C 2118/13.

Army Form C. 2118.

WAR DIARY
or
INTELLIGENCE SUMMARY.
(Erase heading not required.)

Instructions regarding War Diaries and Intelligence Summaries are contained in F. S. Regs., Part II. and the Staff Manual respectively. Title pages will be prepared in manuscript.

Place	Date	Hour	Summary of Events and Information	Remarks and references to Appendices
MERCATEL			The Divisional M.G. Coy. of 50th (NORTHUMBRIAN) DIVISION.	
"	31st Aug. 1st	—	Working at bomb-smelting huts, tents &c. Iman to VII Corps Rest Station-Sick	
"		—	Received O.O. No.115 "A" Coy. not affected by this order. G.S.O.1 visited bomb & informed me the Coy. would not take over positions in the trenches until the 7th inst.	No 2 Operation order G.S.O.1. 50th Div."
"	2nd	—	Received Div'l letter G.X.4025/18 - No23 Div'l M.G. Offr: making all arrangements for 8 guns to go to the lines to relieve S 2, 3, 4, 5, 6, 7, 8, 9 in the intermediate line on the 7th Aug.	No 3 Div'l letter G.S.O.1 50th Div"
"	3rd	—	Saw G.O.C. 150th I.Bde. with D.M.G.O. who arranged for 3 guns to relieve S 5, 6, & 7 on the 3rd inst. 2 Teams No 3 Sect. & 1 Team No 1 Sect: with Lt. A.J. BARNES and 2/LT. PARSONS respectively relieved the britions at 11 p.m.	
"		—	Received O.O. No.116 from Div'l H.Q. regarding transfer of 50th Div. from VII Corps to VI Corps and consequent extension of Div'l front to the right necessitating relieving of part of line held by 21st Division on right by 50th Div's. This was the reason for the sudden order from D.M.G.O. to send 3 guns to relieve S 5 S 6 & S 7.	No 4 Operation order G.S.O.1. 50th Div"
"		—	Orders from D.M.G.O. to send 2 guns on night of 4th inst. to relieve britions S 8 & S 9.	

Army Form C. 2118.

WAR DIARY
or
INTELLIGENCE SUMMARY.
(Erase heading not required.)

Instructions regarding War Diaries and Intelligence Summaries are contained in F. S. Regs., Part II. and the Staff Manual respectively. Title pages will be prepared in manuscript.

Place	Date	Hour	Summary of Events and Information	Remarks and references to Appendices
MERCATEL & Tumulus	AUG. 4.		Sent up 2 Gun Teams under 2/LT. WHEATLEY N°3 Sect. to relieve S & D Sq; at 11 p.m.	Appendix
"	5°		Rec'd orders from D.M.G.O. (N°5) Gun on durs to 2/LIET. G.E. BARNES to take up S2, 3 & 4 positions to be taken over one night 6/7 Aug. Gun on durs to 2/LIET. G.E. BARNES to take up remaining 3 guns of N°1 Sect. on the night of 6° inst.	N°5 Letter D.M.G.O. to 2/O...
"	6°		Rec'd orders from D.M.G.O. (N°5) PARSONS that he would be in charge of S2, 3 & 4 - positions in Right Brigade Area; LIEUT. A J BARNES in charge of S5, 6, 8, 7 on right of Ruin COJEUL & 2/LIEUT WHEATLEY in charge of S8 & 9 on left of Ruin COJEUL - the latter 5 positions being in left Brigade Area. Map (N°6) shows disposition of troops of Coy on night of 6/7° Aug. Informed by D.H.G.O. that Durs, on our left ((12? Div?)) is to make a strong raid on enemy positions & that 2 guns from 6 O.T. will be required to place a barrage on the night of the enemy's positions.	MAP N° 6 (Disposition)
	7°			

WAR DIARY
or
INTELLIGENCE SUMMARY.

(Erase heading not required.)

Army Form C. 2118.

Place	Date	Hour	Summary of Events and Information	Remarks and references to Appendices
MERCATEL & Trenches	7	8 p.m.	LIEUT. J.R. HOUGHTON took up 2 guns of N°2 Sect (in bend) to position previously reconnoitred on night of RIVER COJEUL in SUNKEN ROAD at O.19.a.20.50. ref: MAP N°6.	MAP "A" N°6.
	8	11 a.m.	During practice barrage by all guns fire was opened on night of LANYARD TRENCH (MAP A) isolating that trench from ST. ROHART'S FACTORY. Raid postponed.	
	9	11 a.m.	Practice as above again.	
		7.45 a.m.	Zero hour for Raid. Rapid fire kept up for 90 minutes. Casualties 1 N.C.O. (wounded to C.C.S.) Forwarded suggestion to D.M.G.O. that relief of guns in right sector should take place on night 13/14 Aug, 8 in left sector on night 12/13 Aug. 1 O.R. wounded in EGRET TR.	
	10		Received O.O. N°117 & (50° Div.) handed all officers in trenches considerably handicapped by not being in telephone communication with Divl. H.Q. & Bde H.Q. R.P.L. in the line. Reported same to D.M.G.O. ORGANIZATION. The establishment laid down for a M.G. Coy in the field does not seem sufficient. A Transport officer is required during Open Warfare. Weather. Clear but unsettled. Heavy rain during week - Thunder storms on 9° & 10° Aug. 1 O.R. wounded g.s.w. evacuated to 20 C.C.S.	Operation Order N°7 G.S.O.1 50°Div.

Army Form C. 2118.

WAR DIARY
or
INTELLIGENCE SUMMARY.
(Erase heading not required.)

Instructions regarding War Diaries and Intelligence Summaries are contained in F. S. Regs., Part II. and the Staff Manual respectively. Title pages will be prepared in manuscript.

Place	Date	Hour	Summary of Events and Information	Remarks and references to Appendices
MERCATEL	12th	4 p.m.	Issued Operation Orders for Relief on night 13/14/2.	O.O. No 8 O.O. No 1 O.C. 245 Coy.
	13th		Relief completed 11 p.m.	
	14th		LIEUT. A.J. BARNES proceeded on special leave (10 days).	No 9
	16th		Received Operation Orders from Division.	D.O. No 118 G.S.O.I. 50th Div.
	17th		Conference at 245 MG Coy. HQ. at 12 noon. attended by Div MG O. O.C. 149 O.C. 150 & O.C. 151 P.O.C. 245 MG Coys. Discussed the new Divisional M.G. Defence Scheme — part of the VIth Corps Defence Scheme. Received letter from Div: showing division of gun positions under new Defence Scheme — all guns in front by 6 A.M. 21st Aug. 1 O.R. wounded in EGRET TR.	No 10 50th Div: G.X 4025/34 G.S.O.I.
	18th		Attended VIth Corps Narrow Flour at BIHUCOURT. 1 Entry in Event 18 - pair of nurses	
	19th		Issued Operation Orders for reliefs on nights of 19, 20 & 21st Aug.	No 11 D.O. No 2 O.C. 245 Coy.
	20th		Received Orders from BH.Q.O. that - S3 med not be occupied. Posns occupied by Coy on night of 20/21st - S4, S5, S6, S7, S9, S10, S11 & S12. In position by 6 A.M. 21st Aug. according to Divl letter. - Map showing posn of all HQs in Divl Sector & how divided amongst MG Coys.	No 12 MAP - HQs in Divl Sector
	21st		Relief postponed - gas attack to be released on 50th DIV'L FRONT at 10.30 p.m. Issued Orders for relief to take place on night - 22nd/23rd.	

Army Form C. 2118.

WAR DIARY
or
INTELLIGENCE SUMMARY.
(Erase heading not required.)

Instructions regarding War Diaries and Intelligence Summaries are contained in F. S. Regs., Part II. and the Staff Manual respectively. Title pages will be prepared in manuscript.

Place	Date	Hour	Summary of Events and Information	Remarks and references to Appendices
MERCATEL Sheet 51B. (France) 1/40,000 M.24.C.2.4. & Trenches	22nd		2/Lt. PARSONS (No 1 Sect.) relieved 2/Lt. DERBYSHIRE (No 4 Sect.) in S.4, S.5 2/Lt. BARNES (No 1 Sect.) relieved LIEUT. HOUGHTON (No 2 Sect.) in S.6, S.7. 2/Lt. WHEATLEY (No 3 Sect.) relieved 2/Lt. ATTWATER (No 2 Sect.) in S.8, S.9, S.10, S.11, S.12. Division of Positions: S.4, S.5, S.6. R. BDE. S.7 Rt. of River } L. BDE. S.8, 9, 10, 11, Lt of River }	
	26th		Received operation Orders from Division H.Q. Brigade W/16/5.	N° 13 O.O. N° 118 G.S.O.I. 50th Div.
	27th	8 P.M	CAP. W.R. THOMSON proceeded on leave to U.K. (10 days). Lieut. L.W. REES assumed temporary command of the Company. During the night very violent storm, which came down sheets of rain, several tents were down and sheets of iron displaced.	
	28th	4 P.M	Issued operation orders for reliefs on night of 29/30th Aug 1917 in position S.6.	N° 14 O.O. N° 3 245 M.G. Coy
	29th		2/Lt DERBYSHIRE (No 4 Sec) relieved 2/Lt PARSONS (No 1 Sec) in S.4, S.5. Sgt JENKINS (No 4 Sec) relieved 2/Lt G. BARNES (No 1 Sec) in S.6, S.7 2/Lt ATTWATER (No 2 Sec) relieved 2/Lt WHEATLEY (No 3 Sec) in S.9 S.10, S.11, S.12.	
	30	1 P.M	Lt R.J. HOUGHTON & 1.O.R. proceeded to CAMIERS to run 47" Vickers Gun Course at C.H.Q. S.A. School 50th DIV G.X. 30/60 L. W. Rees Lt for O.C. 245 M.G. Coy.	

WAR DIARY 245 M.G.Coy.
July 14th to Aug 31st 1917.

SHEET 1.

APPENDICES.

No 1	Movement Order by 245 MG Coy. to entrain at Point 6 LE HAVRE midnight 28/29th July and detrain at BOISLEUX-AU-MONT. 10 Officers 176 O.R. 6 Riding Horses 2 H.D. 47 mules.	
		28th July. 17.
No 2	Operation Order G.S.O. 1. 50th Divn. No 115 Copy 23. 150th I. Bde to relieve 149th I. Bde in the VIS and GUEMAPPE Sectors on night 4/5th Aug. 17.	
		1st Aug. 17.
No 3	Divisional Letter G.X. 4025/18 G.S.O. 1. 50th Divn. Divisional MG Coy (245th) take over following positions on 7th inst. S2, S3, S4, S5, S6, S7, S8 & S9. Personnel of 245 MG Coy. to be attached to detachments in the line for instruction. Officers NCO's & men to learn the Divisional Sector as soon as possible.	
		2nd Aug 17.
No 4.	Operation Order No 116 G.S.O. 1 50th Divn. Copy No 21. 1. 50th Divn. transferred from VII Corps to VI Corps at noon 7.8.17. 2. Boundary between 50th Divn. & 21st Divn. (on right) altered 3. 150th I Bde extend to OTTO ALLEY 151st I Bde extend to PUG LANE.	
		3rd Aug. 17.
No 5	Letter re Relief D.M.G.O. 50th Divn. 245 MG Coy. to take over posns S2, 3, & 4 on night 6/7th Aug. 17. S.O. directly responsible to G.O.C. 151 I Bde. (R Sector)	
		5th Aug. 17.
No 6	Trench Map showing disposition of 245 MG Coy on night 6/7th Aug. 17. Showing also positions & target of guns during Raid by 12th Divn. on 9th Aug 17.	
No 7	Operation Order No 117 G.S.O. 1 50th Divn. Copy 20 149th I. Bde to relieve 151st I Bde in CHERISY Sector on night 12/13th Aug. 17.	
		10th Aug. 17.

WAR DIARY 245" M G Coy.
July 14" to Aug. 31st 1917.

SHEET 2.

APPENDICES.

Nº 8	Operation Order Nº 1 (245 MG Coy) attached. Copy 4.	
Nº 9	Operation Order Nº 118 G.S.O. 1 50" Divn Copy 20 151st I. Bde. to relieve 150" I. Bde in VIS and GUEMAPPE Sectors on night 20/21st Aug. 17.	16" Aug. 17.
Nº 10	Divisional Letter G.X. 4025/34 G.S.O. 1 50" Divn 1. Attached Map (App: Nº 12) substituted for previous M.G. Maps. 2. Right Bde. to occupy posns 1 to 7 inclusive & S1 & S2. Left Bde. " " 8 to 15 " & S8 245" M.G. Coy. " " S3 to S7 " & S9 to S12 inclusive Guns to be in position by 6 A.M. Aug. 21st 17. 3. Remaining 7 guns per BDE. M.G. Coy. in the line to be at disposal of G.O.C. BDE.	17" Aug. 17.
Nº 11	Operation Order Nº 2 (245 M.G. Coy) attached Copy 9.	
Nº 12	Map showing M.G.'s in Divn Sector. attached	
Nº 13	Operation Order Nº 119 G.S.O. 1 50" Divn Copy 20. 150" I. Bde to relieve 149" I. Bde in FONTAINE and CHERISY Sectors on night 28/29" Aug. 17.	26" Aug. 17.
Nº 14	Operation Order No 3. (245 M.G. Coy) attached. Copy 4.	

Trench Map. Chérisy Sector. No 6

A Part of FRANCE Sheet 57.B.SW.
1/20,000

Explanation:
- — British Trench
- — German "
- ⬤⟶ M.G. Emplacem't
- ▨ VILLAGE
- — Boundary line

A. Pos'n of 2 guns on 9th Aug. during raid by 12th Div'n on left.

Trench-Map showing Distribution of Guns: on night 6/7th Aug.'17.

5 guns in Left Brigade Sector
  (2 L. of River - 3 R. of River)

3 guns in Right Brigade Sector.

8 guns in Line
8 guns at H.Q. Camp - Mercatel.
___
16 guns.

W.R. Thomson Capt
O.C. 245 M.G.Coy.

SECRET   App. No 8   Copy No 4

OPERATION ORDER No 1
by Capt W.R. Thomson Commdg 245 M.G. Coy.
12° Aug. 17.

Relief. 1. No 2 Sect. will relieve No 3 Sect. in the Left Bde Sector and No 4 Sect. will relieve No 1 Sect. in the Right Bde. Sector on the night 13/14° Aug. 17.

Officers. 2. (a) 2/LT. DERBYSHIRE will take over from 2/LT. PARSONS in S2, S3 & S4.
(b) LT. HOUGHTON will take over from LT. BARNES in S5, S6 & S7.
(c) 2/LT. ATTWATER will take over from 2/LT. WHEATLEY in S8 & S9.

Details. 3. Details of teams to be arranged by Sect. Off. concerned.

No 1's. 4. No 1's of relieving teams will be attached to the team they are relieving 24 hours before the relief.

Guides. 5. Guides will be at—
(a) FOSTER DUMP for S2 & 3 at 10·30 P.M.
(b) SHAWK DUMP for S4, 5, 6, & 7 at 10·30 P.M.
(c) RAKE DUMP for S8 & 9 at 10·45 P.M.
1 Guide per gun.

Tripods. 6. Tripods & Belt Boxes will be taken over.

Limbers. 7. Limbers will if necessary be withdrawn to a safer place than the Dumps & return in time to meet relieved teams.

"Relief Complete" 8. "Relief Complete" to be acknowledged direct to BDE. H.Q. concerned:—
(a) for S2, 3 & 4 (Right Sector) to H.Q. Right Bde.
(b) for S5, 6, 7, 8 & 9 (Left Sector) to H.Q. Left Bde.

Handing Over 9. This Operation Order will be handed over to the relieving Officer.

12° Aug. 1917.

                     W.R. Thomson Capt.
                     O.C. 245 MG Coy.

245 M.G.Coy. OPERATION ORDER No 2

APPENDIX No 11.

SECRET.   19TH AUG. 1917.
Copy No 9.

I. DIVISIONAL SCHEME.

The new Divisional M.G. Defence Scheme will come into force at 6 A.M. 21st Aug. by which time all guns must be in position.

II. POSITIONS: DIV'L M.G.COY.

The Divisional (No 245) M.G.Coy. will take over position in the Support Lines as follows:—

SECTOR	SUB-SECTOR	No	OLD No	MAP. REF'CE.	TRENCH.
RIGHT BRIGADE		S 3		N.36.a.70.45	BOTHAM
	→	S 4	S 2	N.30.c.90.60	BOTHAM ROOKERY
		S 6	S 4	N.30.b.60.40	EGRET LOOP
LEFT BRIGADE	Right of River	S 7	S 6	O.19.c.25.05	EGRET
	LEFT OF RIVER COTJUL	S 9	S 8	N.13.d.08.95	RAKE
		S 10		O.13.b.30.80	RAKE
		S 11		do	do
		S 12		do	do

Hereafter in this Order the new No will be used followed when possible by the old No in brackets.

III. RELIEFS. 19/20TH AUG.

A. RIGHT SECTOR.
    NIL.

B. LEFT SECTOR   1. RIGHT OF RIVER

(I). The team of No 2 Sect? in S.8. (S.7) will be relieved by a team of 151. M.G.Coy.

(II). 1 Guide for S.8.(S.7) & 1 Guide for Officer H.Q. in LION TRENCH to be at junction of SHIKAR AVENUE with EGRET TRENCH (O.19.C. 65.80) at 10.30.p.m.

(III). Relieved team under Sgt. SAVILLE to return to Camp. ½ Limber will be at SUNKEN ROAD (O.19.a.10.60) at 11.30.p.m.

(IV). No 1 to remain behind with relieving team. Report to LT HOUGHTON at 9.A.M.

(V). LIEUT HOUGHTON will be relieved by an Officer of 151. M.G.Coy. and will move to the O.P. behind S.7.(S.6).

2. LEFT OF RIVER.

(I). The team of No 2 Sect? in present S.9. will relieve the team of 150 M.G.Coy. in S.10.

(II). Details of relief to be arranged between 2/LT. ATTWATER & Officer of 150 M.G.Coy.

(III). "Relief Complete" to H.Q. L. Bde.

IV. RELIEFS 20/21ST AUG.

A. RIGHT SECTOR

(I). The team of No 4 Sect? in present S.3. will move to S.4 (BOTHAM TRENCH. above AVENUE TRENCH.) S.A.A. will be taken. OLD S.3 will be abandoned.

(II). "Occupied" to be sent to H.Q. R. Bde.

B. LEFT SECTOR.   1. RIGHT OF RIVER.

~~The team of No 4 Sec. in S.5.(old) will return to Camp without relief. S.5 will be abandoned. S.A.A. will be taken from S.7 (S.6). ½ Limber will be at SHAWK DUMP at 9.30.P.M. (Ration Limber).~~

Cancelled. See attached slip
The above paragraph again holds good.

2. LEFT OF RIVER.
(i). 2 teams of No 3 Sec. will take over S.11 & S.12.
(ii). Guides provided by 2/Lt. ATTWATER at RAKE DUMP. 10.P.M.
(iii). 2/Lt. WHEATLEY will occupy the TUNNEL at S.11 & S.12.
(iv). "Relief Complete" to H.Q. L.B.de.

V. RELIEFS. 21/22nd AUG.

A. RIGHT SECTOR.
(i). Teams of No 4 Sec in S.4, S.5.(S.2.) & S.6.(S.4) will be relieved by teams of No 1 SEC.
(ii). 2/Lt. PARSONS will take over from 2/Lt. DERBYSHIRE at the ROOKERY. The latter to return to Camp with his 3 teams.
(iii). Guides for S.4 & S.5.(S.2) to be on Ration Road (ROTTEN ROW) at a place to be fixed by 2/Lt. DERBYSHIRE.
Limber will go on until it meets them 10.30.P.M.
GUIDE for S.6.(S.4) at SHAWK DUMP. 10.P.M.
(iv). "Relief Complete" to H.Q. R.B.de.

B. LEFT SECTOR.   1. RIGHT OF RIVER.
(i). The team of No 2 Sec. in S.7.(S.6) will be relieved by a team of No 1 SEC.
(ii). 2/Lt G.E BARNES will take over from LT HOUGHTON at O.P. behind S.7.(S.6). The latter will return to Camp with his team.
(iii). Guide at SHAWK DUMP 10.P.M.
iv. "RELIEF COMPLETE" TO H.Q. L.B.de.

2. LEFT OF RIVER.
(i). The teams of No 2 Sec. in S.9.(S.8) & S.10 will be relieved by 2 teams of No 3 SEC.
(ii). Relieved teams under 2/Lt ATTWATER will return to Camp.
(iii). Guides at RAKE DUMP. 10.P.M.
(iv). Relief Complete to H.Q. L.B.de.

VI. TRIPODS, BELT BOXES &c

In Company relief these will be taken over by the relieving teams.
When relieved by another Coy. they will be taken over & when relieving another Coy. they will be taken over.

W.P.Thomson Captain
Aug 14th 1917   OC 248 M.G.Coy

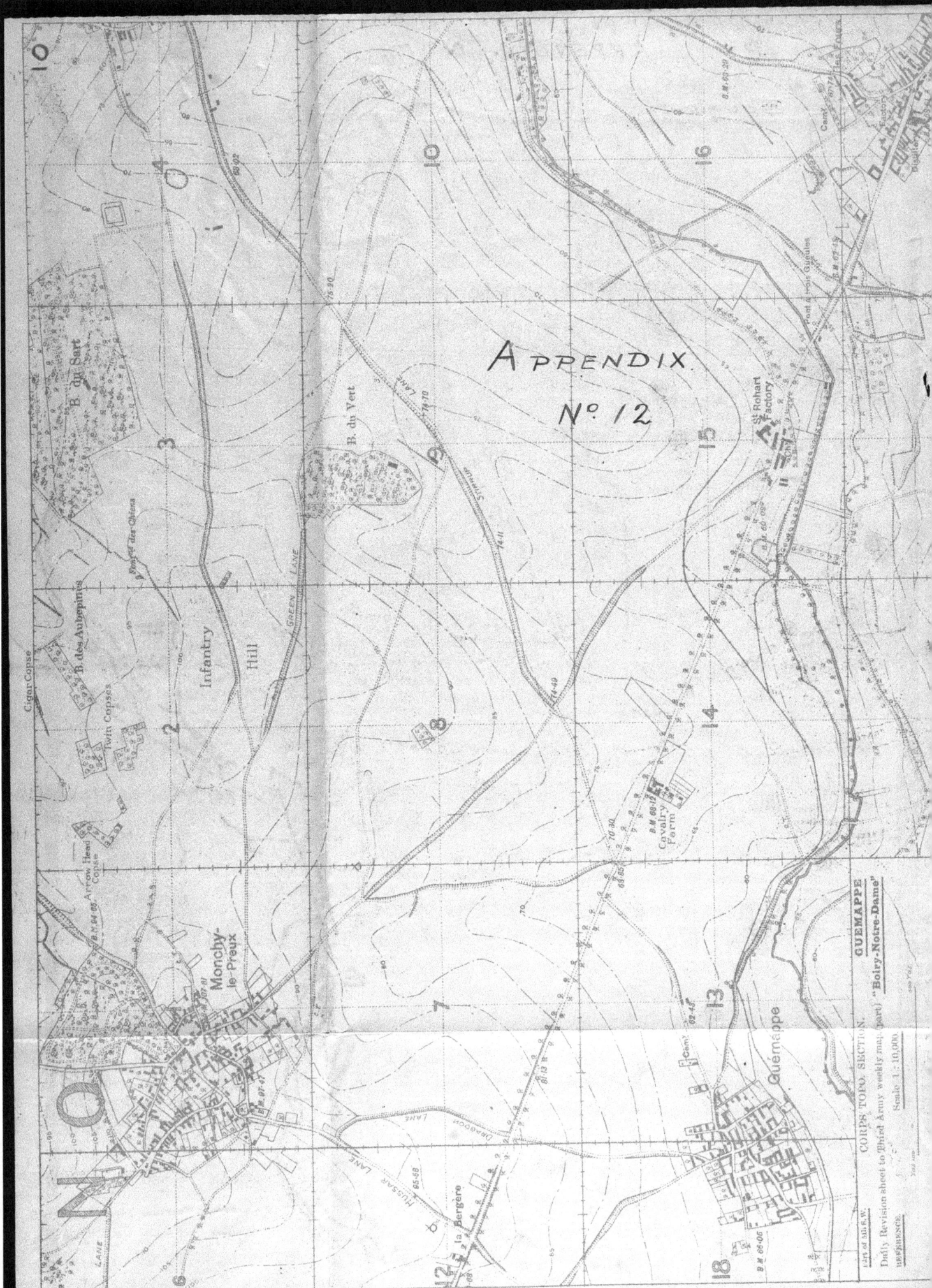

Appendix 14.   COPY No 4

Operation Order No 3.
by
Captain W. R. Thomson
Commanding No 245 M.G. Coy.

RELIEFS.   29/30 Aug. 1917.   28th Aug. 1917.
            RIGHT BRIGADE.
            No. 4 Section will relieve No. 1 Section at
            the ROOKERY. POSITIONS S.4. S.5. S.6.

            LEFT BRIGADE.
            No. 2 Section will relieve No. 3 Section in
            the LEFT BRIGADE area. POSITIONS S.7. S.9.
            S.10. S.11. S.12.

OFFICERS.   2/LT. DERBYSHIRE. will take over from
            2/LT. PARSONS. at the ROOKERY.
            POSITIONS. S.4. S.5
            The latter to return to camp with his teams
            Sgt JENKINS.
            ~~2/Lt ATTWATER~~ will take over from
            2/LT. G.E. BARNES. in the LEFT SECTOR
            RIGHT OF RIVER. POSITIONS S.6 & S.7.
            The latter to return to camp with his teams.

            2/LIEUT ATTWATER ~~HOUGHTON~~ will take over from
            2/LT. WHEATLEY. in the LEFT SECTOR
            LEFT OF RIVER. POSITIONS. S.9. S.10. S.11. S.12.
            The latter to return to camp with his teams.

TEAMS.   Details of teams will be arranged by
            Section Officers.

RELIEF   Relief complete will be communicated
COMPLETE.   to H.Q's BRIGADE CONCERNED.

        THIS O.O. TO BE HANDED TO RELIEVING
        OFFICER.
                                    L W Rees Lt.
                                    for CAPTAIN.
                            O.C. No 245 M.G.Coy.

ORIGINAL

Vol 3

CONFIDENTIAL

÷ WAR DIARY ÷

÷ OF ÷

÷ 245 MACHINE GUN COMPANY ÷

From 1st Sept. 1917 To 30th Sept. 1917.

[VOLUME 2]

Army Form C. 2118.

Sheet 1.

WAR DIARY
or
INTELLIGENCE SUMMARY.

(Erase heading not required.)

Instructions regarding War Diaries and Intelligence Summaries are contained in F.S. Regs., Part II. and the Staff Manual respectively. Title pages will be prepared in manuscript.

Place	Date	Hour	Summary of Events and Information	Remarks and references to Appendices
MERCATEL. REF O.S.France. SHEET 51B. M.24.c.2.4	3.9.17	9:30 A.M	Received 50th Div O.O. No. 120.	App. 1.
	5th	6pm	Issued Coy O.O. No 4 for the relief of No 2 & 4 Sections on night of 6/7th	" 2
	6th		D.H.Q.O informed with numbering of Emplacements according to map. Received 50th Div Letter G.X.4025/43 numbering Emplacements under VI Corps Defence Scheme. No 1 Sect. relieving No 4 Coys in pos. S4, 5, 6,7 in CHERISY SECTOR. No 3 Sect. relieved No 2 Sect. in pos. S9, 10, 11,12,13 in GUEMAPPE SECTOR. Nos 2 & 4 Sects. returned to Camp.	" 3
	8th		Received Appendix Nos 1 to 50th Div. O.O. No 121 (received no copy of O.O No 121). Coy. H.Q & Reserve Sections moved to CARLISLE CAMP M.16. (Hutin Camp). Transport moved to temporary lines 200y N. of CARLISLE CAMP awaiting erection of WINTER STANDINGS. Capt. W.R. THOMSON returned from leave.	" 4
CARLISLE CAMP.	9th			
	11th		Received 50th Div. O.O. No 122.	" 5
	12th		LIEUT. A.J. BARNES returned from leave. Leave had been extended to 11th Sept. 17 by W.O. on Medical Grounds.	
	13th		Issued Coy O.O. No 5 giving M.G. programme for Raid on 13th Sept & giving orders for relief on night 16/17th. night.	" 6

WAR DIARY
or
INTELLIGENCE SUMMARY.

Army Form C. 2118.

Sheet 2.

Place	Date	Hour	Summary of Events and Information	Remarks and references to Appendices
CARLISLE CAMP	14"		LT. A.J. BARNES to Hospital. Heard orders giving ZERO hours for Raid on 15-2 unit. Nos 2 & 4 Sectns (Raising Coln) moved up to positions Chosen & Constructed during week for giving barrage fire during Raid.	Appx 7.
	15"		A Batt. of 50° Div° raided enemy trenches opposite CHERISY. Details ors given in Appendix. M.G.'s fired according to programme. Enemy retaliated on DUCK TRENCH with 10.5 cm. Shells - 3 men slightly wounded. Forced to withdraw 1, 2 & 3 guns of E Group from DUCK TRENCH at 8 p.m. owing to heavy enemy shell fire. Enemy also retaliated with 15 cm. shells in RAKE TRENCH. No casualties.	Appx 8.
	16"		No. 4 Sectn relieved No. 1 Sectn in posns 50A, 51A, 52A & 53A in the CHERISY SECTOR. No. 2 Sectn relieved No. 3 Sectn in posns 59A & 61(3guns) in the GUÉMAPPE SECTOR. Nos 1 & 3 Section returned to Camp.	
	19"		Received O.O. No. 123 (50" Div") 2/LT. G.E. BARNES to Hospital Trench Fever.	Appx 9.

Army Form C. 2118.

Sheet 3

WAR DIARY
or
INTELLIGENCE SUMMARY.
(Erase heading not required.)

Place	Date	Hour	Summary of Events and Information	Remarks and references to Appendices
CARLISLE CAMP	21st		Issued Coy. O.O. No 6.	App.x 10
	23rd		No 1 Sect. relieved No 4 Sect. in CHERISY SECTOR - No 4 Sect. returned to Camp/s	
			No 2 " " No 2 " - GUEMAPPE " - No 2 " "	
			No 3 " "	
	24th		Attended Meeting of Divisional Committee for Winter Sports. Preliminary Competitions to start as soon as Division is out of the line. D.M.G.O. came to Camp to explain details of Scheme for Gassing certain Areas in German line - M.G.s to co-operate in bombardment. Received no orders from Divl. H.Q.	
	25th		Received Divl. Warning Order No 124.	Appx 11
			Received Divl. letter G.X.4555/4. 2/Lt. PARSONS visited ROOKERY & explained Scheme to him. Bombardment to take place at 5 A.M.	Appx 12A
			On returning to CAMP received G X 4555/3 delaying events.	" 12
			Received wire postponing bombardment - & took from D.M.G.O. that 2/Lt. PARSONS had been warned.	
	26th		Saw D.M.G.O. re new programme of M.G. fire and map of areas to be bombarded - him should have accompanied G X 4555/3.	
	27th	5 AM	Bombardment & gas took place MGs cooperating.	Appx 14
			Issued Coy. O.O. No 7.	Appx 13
			Received Divl. O.O. No 125.	

Army Form C. 2118.

Sheet 4.

WAR DIARY
or
INTELLIGENCE SUMMARY.
(Erase heading not required.)

Instructions regarding War Diaries and Intelligence Summaries are contained in F. S. Regs., Part II. and the Staff Manual respectively. Title pages will be prepared in manuscript.

Place	Date	Hour	Summary of Events and Information	Remarks and references to Appendices
CARLISE CAMP	Sept. 28°		Received Div'l Ltr No GX 4586. M.G. Co-operation required in bombardment of new enemy trench. Gave orders to 2/Lt. PARSONS to perform task as at No 9. 18th 9° M.G. Coy. LT. HOUGHTON returned from M.G. School CAMIERS.	App:x 15
	29°		Discussed Scheme with 149 MG Coy. Gave 2/Lt. PARSONS orders to fire 2 guns in CUCKOO RESERVE TRENCH. Postponed relief of N°1 Sect by N° 4 Sect 24 hr. Bombardment took place with M.G.'s co-operating. Received Div'l O.O. N° 126	App:x 16
	30°		N° 2 Sect: relieved N° 3 Sect: in GUEMAPPE Sector. N° 3 Sect: returned to camp	
			Weather: Uniformly fine throughout the month. No rain. Much work carried out in consequence. Trenches, emplacements, billets &c in excellent condition	

LR Thomson Capt
O/C 245 M.G. Coy.

1.

APPENDICES TO WAR DIARY OF
245 MACHINE GUN COMPANY FROM 1ST SEPT. to 30TH SEPT. 17.

Appendix No	Subject & Author.
1	50TH Divn. O.O. No 120 2.9.17. Copy 20. 149th I. Bde. to relieve 151st I. Bde. in Left Sector (VIS à GUEMAPPE) on night 5/6th Sept. G.S. 50th Divn.
2 attached	Coy. O.O. No 4 5.9.17. (attached) O.C. 245 MG Coy.
3	50TH Divn. Letter GX 4025/43 5.9.17. 1. Positions of M.G's in Divl Sector as laid down in VI Corps Defence Scheme (M.G.) shown in Map. 2. Distribution (C) 245th M.G. Coy. 50A, 51A, 52A, 53A, 59A, 61 (3 guns). G.S. 50th Divn.
3A	Map showing M.G. postns under VI Corps M.G. Defence Scheme.
4	Appendix No 1 to 50th Divn. O.O. No 121. 7.9.17. Copy 6. Machine Gun Programme for Raid opposite CHERISY. All details of this Programme are given in Appendix 6. G.S. 50th Divn.
5	50th Divn. O.O. No 122 10.9.17. Copy 20. 151st I. Bde. to relieve 150th I. Bde. in Right Sector (CHERISY) on night 13/14th Sept. G.S. 50th Divn.
6 attached	Coy. O.O. No 5. 12.9.17. Copy 7. (attached) O.C. 245 M.G. Coy.
7 attached	Coy. Letter giving Zero Hours &c for Raid opposite CHERISY. (attached) O.C. 245 MG Coy.
8 attached	50TH Divn. Intelligence Summary giving Report on Raid opposite CHERISY on 15.9.17. (attached) 16.9.17. G.S. 50th Divn.
9	50th Divn. O.O. No 123 19.9.17. Copy 20 150th I. Bde. to relieve 149th I. Bde. in Left Sector (VIS à GUEMAPPE) on night 21/22nd Sept. G.S. 50th Divn.
10 attached	Coy. O.O. No 6. 21.9.17 Copy 6 (attached). O.C. 245 M.G. Coy.

APPENDICES TO WAR DIARY OF
245 MACHINE GUN COMPANY FROM 1st Sept. to 30th Sept '17.

Appendix No.	Subject & Author
11	50th Divn. WARNING ORDER No. 124. 25.9.17 Copy 22 1. 50th Divn. less Artillery will be relieved with two by 51st Divn. less artillery by October 6th. 2. On relief 50th Divn. will move to VI Corps Southern Reserve Divl Area (COURCELLES - GOMMIECOURT & ACHIET-LE-PETIT). 3. Detailed orders will be issued later. G.S. 50th Divn.
12	50th Divn. Letter G X 4555/3 24.9.17. 1. Gas to be projected on CHERISY, HILLSIDE WORK, CHALK PIT, on 26.9.17. 2. Zero 5 a.m. 3. Smoke & gas shell bombardment. 4. D.M.G.O. to arrange for M.G. barrages on areas to be gassed from Zero to Zero + 15 mins. 5. "RUBBISH" to mean postponement. G.S. 50th Divn.
12A	50th Divn. Letter GX 4555/4 25.9.17. Zero to be between 4·45 & 5·15 A.M. If operation is postponed & weather again appears favourable "WANCOURT" to mean operation in execution at same time following morning.
13	50th Divn. O.O. No. 125 26.9.17. Copy 20. 149th I. Bde to relieve 151st I. Bde in Right Sector (CHERISY) on night 29/30th Sept. 1917. G.S. 50th Divn.
14 attached	Coy. O.O. No. 7. 27.9.17. Copy 6. O.C. 245 M.G. Coy.

15	50th Divn. Letter GX 4586 28.9.17.
	1. Concentration of 18 pdrs, M.G.'s & STOKES Mortars on enemy's new trench in O.20.B.7.d. on night 29/30th or 1st. Subsequent night on which a working party is reported in it.
	2. Oblique M.G. fire from SW & NW to be arranged by D.M.G.O.
	3. Zero hour to be taken for MG's on opening of 18 pdr barrage.
	   Zero to Zero + 3 mins 1 belt/min.
	   Zero + 3 to Zero + 5 mins 1 belt/2 mins.
	   Zero + 30 to Zero + 36 mins. 1 belt/2 mins.
	4. If postponed "ROT" to be sent to all concerned.
	G.S. 50th Divn.

APPENDICES TO WAR DIARY OF
245 MACHINE GUN COMPANY FROM 1st Sept. to 30: Sept. 1917

Appendix No	Subject & Author
	50TH DIVn O.O. No 126 29.9.17. Copy 22 1 50TH Divn front to be held in future by one Bde. permanently allotted to LEFT SECTOR, the other 2 Bdes. relieving one another alternately in RIGHT SECTOR. 2 Re. distribution. (Divl M.G. Coy not affected by this order as regards M.G.'s in the defensive line.) G.S. 50: Divn

1st Oct. 1917.

L R Thomson Capt-
O.C. 245 M.G. Coy.

Appendix 2.

OPERATION ORDER No 4. Copy No 2

No 245 M.G. Coy.   Sept 5th 1917.

Secret

RELIEFS 6/7 SEPT. 1917.

RIGHT BRIGADE No 1 SECTION WILL RELIEVE No 4
SECTION AT THE ROOKERY. POSITIONS. S.4. S.5. S.6.
position S.7 left Brigade
LEFT BRIGADE No 3 SECTION WILL RELIEVE No 2
SECTION IN LEFT BRIGADE AREA. POSITIONS.
S.11. S.9. S.10. S.11. S.12.

OFFICERS. 2/LT. PARSONS WILL TAKE OVER FROM
2/LT. DERBYSHIRE AT THE ROOKERY. POSITIONS. S.4.S.5.
THE LATTER TO RETURN TO CAMP WITH HIS TEAMS.

2/LT. G.E. BARNES WILL TAKE OVER FROM
Cpl. JENKINS IN LEFT SECTOR. RIGHT OF RIVER.
POSITIONS S.6. S.7.
THE LATTER TO RETURN TO CAMP WITH HIS TEAMS.

2/LT. WHEATLEY WILL TAKE OVER FROM
2/LT. ATTWATER. IN LEFT SECTOR. LEFT OF RIVER.
POSITIONS. S.9. S.10. S.11. S.12.
THE LATTER TO RETURN TO CAMP WITH HIS TEAMS.

TEAMS. DETAILS OF TEAMS WILL BE ARRANGED
BY SECTION OFFICERS.

RELIEFS COMPLETE TO BE COMMUNICATED TO H. Qrs.
BRIGADE CONCERNED.

AMMUNITION. 6 BOXES S.A.A. AND 14 BELT BOXES
7 OF WHICH WILL BE DEFINITELY ALLOTTED
TO FIRING ON S.O.S. LINES FROM BATTLE
POSITIONS WILL HENCEFORTH BE KEPT AT
EACH POSITION. RELIEVING TEAMS ON NIGHT
6/7 WILL TAKE UP THE REQUISITE NUMBER OF
BELT BOXES TO COMPLETE.

FIRE. ALL GUNS ARE AVAILABLE FOR HARASSING
FIRE AT THE DISCRETION OF THE BRIGADE
CONCERNED AND ORDERS IN REGARD THERETO
WILL USUALLY BE CONVEYED THROUGH THE
O.C. BRIGADE M.G. Coy. THE FOLLOWING
LIMITATIONS WILL HOWEVER BE OBSERVED.

(A) GUNS WILL NOT FIRE FROM S.O.S. BATTLE Posn

(B) GUNS WILL NOT BE MOVED FURTHER
THAN 300 YARDS FROM THEIR BATTLE POSITIONS.

(C) IN THE EVENT OF ATTACK THEY WILL
RETURN TO BATTLE POSITIONS AND OPEN
ON THEIR S.O.S. LINES.

(D) THE SUPPLY OF S.A.A. VIZ. 6 BOXES S.A.A.
& 14 BELT BOXES MUST BE MAINTAINED
AT ALL TIMES.

L.W. Rees
fr CAPTAIN
O.C. 245. M.G. Coy

Appendix 6.   **SECRET**
                                                    Sheet 1.

Operation Order No 5 by Captn W. R. THOMSON
          Commdg 245 M.G. Coy.

                                    12th Septr 1917.
                                    Copy No 7

Refce Trench Map 1/10,000 VIS-EN-ARTOIS (Sheet 51 B S.W.)

1.   A Battalion of the 50th Divn will raid NARROW TRENCH between O.26.C.50.70 and O.32.a.25.95 on 15th Sept. 17 – depth of 200 yds.

2.   There will be 3 PHASES in the RAID – the ZERO hour for each will be notified later.

3.   The following Groups will be supplied by 245 M.G. Coy :–

Group	No of Guns	Position	Section
B1	4	BROWN TR.	No 2
E	8	DUCK TR.	No 1 &
			No 4
K	3	RAKE TR.	No 3

4.   Officers concerned will reconnoitre their positions and make suitable firing emplacements.
        All guns to be in position by 12 NOON on ZERO day.

5.   One Officer from each group will attend at the WESTERN entrance of FOSTER AVENUE at 12 NOON on ZERO day to check watches.

6.   All guns will remain in these positions till 6 A.M. on ZERO +1 day at which hour they will begin to resume their normal positions.

7.   Programme of Firing.
        (a) B1 & E GROUPS.

FIRST PHASE
    ZERO   open fire   Zero to Zero+5 mins. 1 belt per min.
                                 Zero+5 to Zero+30 mins. 1 belt per 2 mins.
                                 Zero+30 to Zero+35 mins. 1 belt per min.
                                 Zero+35 to Zero+45 mins. 1 belt per 2mins.
    ZERO+45 mins.   Cease fire.
[NOTE : From Zero+15 to Zero+30   4 guns of E Group will fire at a time.]

SECOND PHASE
    ZERO   open fire   Zero to Zero+5 mins. 1 belt per min.
                                 Zero+5 to Zero+25 mins. 1 belt per 2 mins.
    ZERO+25 mins.   Cease fire.

THIRD PHASE
    ZERO+20 mins.   open fire   Zero+20 to Zero+25 mins. 1 belt per min.
    ZERO+25 mins.   cease fire.

        (b) K GROUP

FIRST PHASE
    ZERO   open fire   Zero to Zero+5 mins. 1 belt per min.
    ZERO+5 mins.   cease fire.

SECOND & THIRD PHASES.
    NIL.

8.   Officers will report to the D.M.G.O. ("FILE") at H.Q. 151 I. Bde ("BROWN") when their guns are in position & ready to fire.

9.   During the night ZERO/ZERO+1day the S.O.S. lines of all guns will be the same as those during the raid. All guns will be on S.O.S. positions.

                                                        P.T.O.

Sheet 2.

10. APPENDICES : TARGETS & GUN POSITIONS

   (i) B1 GROUP   Issued to 2/Lt. ATTWATER
   (ii) E "   (a) " " 2/Lt. DERBYSHIRE
                (b) " " 2/Lt. PARSONS.
                (c) " " 2/Lt. BARNES.
   (iii) K "   " " 2/Lt. WHEATLEY.

11. RELIEFS. Night of 16/17th Sept: 17.

(a)   No. 2 Sect: will relieve No. 3 Sect: in Pos:ns (3 guns) and 59 A – RAKE TRENCH (Left Sector).

        No. 3 Sect: will return to CAMP meeting a guide at the junction of the road from WANCOURT – NEUVILLE VITASSE with the BEAURAINS – NEUVILLE-VITASSE – HENIN-SUR-COJEUL road (in NEUVILLE VITASSE).

        2/Lt. ATTWATER will take over from 2/Lt. WHEATLEY

        "Relief complete" to be reported to H.Q. Left Bde.

(b)   No. 4 Sect: will occupy after the raid Pos:ns 50A (BOTHAM) 51A (ROOKERY), 52A (EGRET LOOP), 53A (EGRET) occupied before the raid by No. 1 Sect:

        No. 1 Sect: will return to camp – a 2nd. guide will be at the point given above in (a).

        2 Limbers will be at SHAWK DUMP at 8.30 p.m.

(c)   Any necessary details to be arranged between Officers concerned.

(d)   "Relief Complete" to be reported to :-
        for 50A, 51A, 52A   to H.Q. Right Bde.
        for 53A   to H.Q. Left Bde.

                                                  Capt:
                                         O.C. 245 M.G. Coy.

Copies to :-

1. 2/Lt. ATTWATER.
2. "   DERBYSHIRE
3. "   PARSONS.
4. "   BARNES.
5. "   WHEATLEY.
6. OFFICE.
7. WAR DIARY ✓
8. WAR DIARY.

[Coy. Operation Order No. 5.]

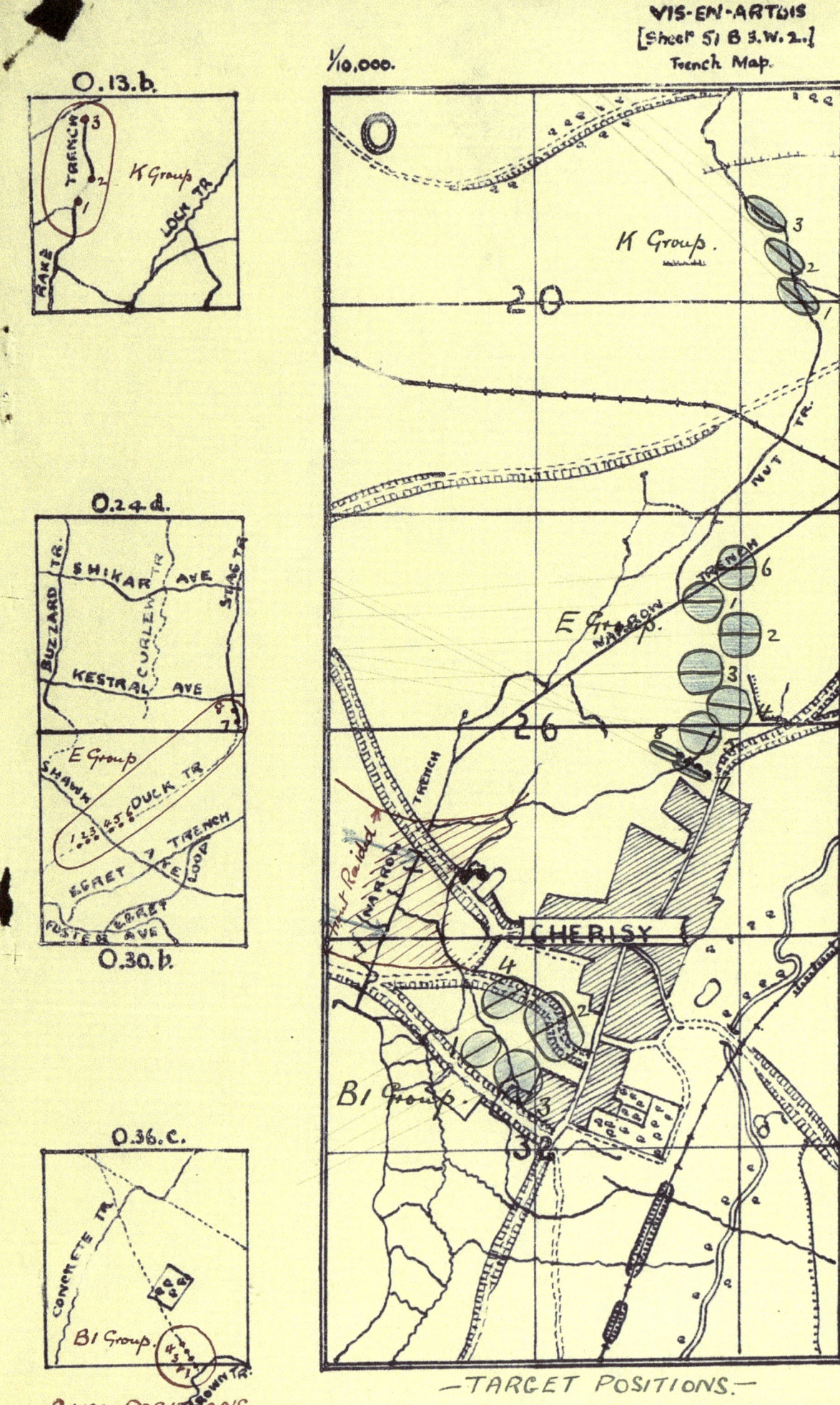

MAPS SHOWING GUNS AND TARGETS FOR RAID.

APPENDIX to 245 Coy. O.O. Nº 5 dated 13th Sept. 17.

ZERO HOURS   Appendix 7.
              Copy No 7
         SECRET.

Ref. O.O. No 5 Para 2

1. ZERO day will be Saturday 15.9.17.
2. 1ST. PHASE   ZERO 4 p.m.
3. 2ND. PHASE   "   7-40 p.m.
4. 3RD. PHASE   "   between 3 A.M. &
   4 A.M. 16.9.17.
   (a) Actual discharge of projectiles will be taken as ZERO. This discharge can easily be seen, and will take place from near junction of FOSTER AVENUE – BULLFINCH SUPPORT.
   (b) If the projectiles are not fired between 3 A.M. & 4 A.M. they will not be fired at all.
5. Should the forecast be quite unfavourable for the projection of gas the word "RATS" will be sent to all concerned. This will mean "3RD PHASE cancelled"

                    W R Thomson Capt.
14.9.17.   O.C. 245 MG Coy.
Copies to all recipients
of O.O. No 5.

GERMAN OFFICIAL. Sept 16TH

Western Front. S.E. of ARRAS enemy artillery activity increased in intensity. Under cover of a smoke cloud the English attacked in the neighbourhood of CHERISY on a front of 1500 Metres. Tanks and flame projectors cleared the way for the assaulting troops but our excellent resistance by artillery and machine guns broke down the attack. In those places where the enemy penetrated into our lines they were ejected in hand to hand fights by our infantry. Towards evening the enemy again attacked at the same point. This undertaking also failed and they were driven back with great loss!!

Appendix 8. War Diary.

50th. DIVISION INTELLIGENCE SUMMARY No.102.

From 12 Noon 15.9.17 to 12 Noon 16.9.17.

A. **INFORMATION ABOUT OURSELVES.**

1. **Operations.**

A Minor operation was successfully carried out on the enemy's trenches, front and support lines, West of CHERISY, in three phases.

(1) 1st. Phase.   A raid at 4 p.m.   ⎫
(2) 2nd. Phase.   A raid at 7.40 p.m.   ⎬ 15th. instant.
(3) Gas attack with projectors at 4.0 a.m. 16th. instant.

1. **First Raid.** Objective NARROW Trench (O.26.c.30.15 to O.26.c.45.75.) and NARROW SUPPORT, (O.26.c.55.05. to O.26.c.90.75.)

Three Companies of the 9th. Durh. L.I. left our front line at 4.0 p.m. behind a most effective artillery barrage, and proceeded to objectives, which were gained with little resistance. Raiders estimate that about 70 of the enemy were killed and 25 prisoners were taken. The R.Es. accompanying the party successfully blew in 11 dugout shafts. The Raiders made a perfect withdrawal at 4.30 p.m. Enemy put down a barrage on our front and Support lines, opposite area raided from 4.5 p.m. till 4.45 p.m. and damaged our trenches.

2. **Second Raid.** Objective Left-third of former objective.

One Company of 8th. Durh.L.I. left our front line at 7.40 p.m. and proceeded to objective behind an equally effective barrage. Very few men were found in the trenches, and were disposed of. Three prisoners were taken, two of whom were killed during the return. One wounded prisoner and two machine guns were brought back to our lines. Raiders withdrew at 8.0 p.m. Enemy put down his barrage very quickly on the same areas as before and continued for about 30 minutes.

Gas Attack. At 4.4. a.m. 552 Gas Drums were successfully projected into enemy lines. At 4.14 a.m. our 18-pdrs. opened intense fire for 10 minutes. Then our 4.5" Hows. opened fire with Lethal Shell on SUN and MOON QUARRIES.

2. **Artillery.**

Harassing fire on enemy's trenches in O.21.a., O.21.b. and O.21.c. Sniping targets engaged as follows :-
5.30 p.m.   Party of 6 at O.28.b.4.5. dispersed; also a party of 3 near STAR CORNER.
6.20 and 6.50 p.m. Two small parties at O.34.a.25.60.
5.40 p.m.   5 men with 2 machine guns in shell hole at O.28.c.7.1.- a direct hit was obtained and casualties inflicted.
6.40 p.m.   Party of men fully equipped in O.26.c.4.4.

At 4.0 p.m. barrage put down on NARROW Trench by 18-pdrs. and at the same time 4.5" hows. opened on their allotted targets. Barrage very satisfactory, shrapnel bursting well with very few high bursts. Enemy retaliation commenced at 4.4. p.m. somewhat ragged and not exceptionally heavy.
7.40 p.m.   Barrage opened. Enemy replied at 7.43 p.m. with considerably heavier fire than in Phase 1. Our Barrage reported very satisfactory.

Enemy tracks and approaches harassed with bursts of fire throughout the night.
1.5 a.m. Working party fired on at O.14.b.7.4.
4.15 a.m.   Batteries fired as ordered in Phase 3. Practically no retaliation.

3. **Defence.** In the Right Section work was chiefly done on revetting and boarding of C.Ts.

In the Left Section a good deal of energy was expended

on improving forward trenches.

4. **Activity.** During 1st. and 2nd. Phases of Operations M.Gs. fired on prearranged lines.

T.Ms. fired in Phases 1.and 2. with very satisfactory results.

A good deal of night harassing firing was done. Hostile aircraft were engaged.

B. INFORMATION ABOUT THE ENEMY.

1. **Artillery.** SENTINEL area and N.34.d. heavily shelled by 10.5 cm. and 15 cm. till 2.30 p.m.   Practically no shelling   in back areas while the various Phases of the raid were in progress and no attempts at counter battery work were made.
Counter Battery. From noon to 2.30 p.m., battery positions in N.34.d. was heavily shelled with 15cm.
O.31.a. shelled with 15 cms.
Front line and Supports in O.26.a.,T.5.a., EGRET and DUCK Trenches shelled with 10.5 cms.
Enemy barrage during raid.
First Phase.   This was laid down 4 minutes after Zero with 10.5 cm. and heavy T.Ms. firing into O.25.d. and O.31.b. Later the enemy fire extended into O.25.c. and d. and STARLING AVENUE.
4.50 p.m. Shelling reported in O.25.b. and d. and O.31.b. with T.Ms., 10.5 cm. at slow rate of fire.
4.55 p.m.   Just an occasional round fired.
The heavy barrage may be said to have slackened very considerably about 4.40 p.m.
A Heavy barrage was put on SHIKAR AVENUE from the front line as far back as LION Trench and considerable damage was done to this C.T.   The Barrage extended as far as the COJEUL RIVER.
BOIRY NOTRE DAME artillery co-operated. It included a 15 cm. How. which barraged SHIKAR AVENUE at O.19.b.9.9.
A 7.7 cm. (either single gun or a section) in VIS-EN-ARTOIS maintained a slow and inaccurate barrage on BUCK RESERVE.
Minenwerfers, which were still in action, kept up a very erratic barrage on the front and support trenches.   There seemed to be very little M.G. fire.
Second Phase. Enemy barrage laid down 3 mins after Zero., heavier than before.   An intense barrage was also put up along SWIFT SUPPORT.
Third Phase. There was no retaliation except for a few T.Ms. on the Support trenches and 7.7 cm. in FOSTER AVENUE.
2. **Movements in enemy's lines and organisation in rear.**
After 3rd. Phase enemy was seen carrying many casualties away on stretchers and handcarts.
No peculiar movment has been observed. Parties were seen on the usual tracks.

3. **General.**
Reference Annex to 50 Div. Int. Summary No. 102.
Under Detailed organisation (page 2, line 19.) for O.26.c.75.65. read O.26.d.75.65.
The SCHMIDTHOHLE.
A large dressing station is stated by prisoners to be in the SCHMIDTHOHLE.
It appears that some troops of the resting Batallion of 76. R.I.R. are also accommodated in same.

[signature]
Lieut. for Lt.-Col,
General Staff,
50th. Division.

16th. September 1917.

Appendix 10.

SECRET

Operation Order No 6 by Capt W.R. Thomson
Commdg 245 M.G. Coy.

21st Sept. 1917.
Copy No 6.

---

1.   (a) No 1 Sect will relieve No 4 Sect in M.G. positions 51A, 52A, 53A (Right Sector) & 54A (Left Sector) on the night 23/24th Sept. 17.

2/Lt. PARSONS will relieve 2/Lt. DERBYSHIRE in the ROOKERY.

(b) No 3 Sect will relieve No 2 Sect in M.G. positions 59A & 61 (3 guns) (Left Sector) on the night 23/24th Sept. 17.

2/Lt. WHEATLEY will relieve 2/Lt. ATTWATER in RAKE TRENCH.

2.   "Relief Complete" will be reported to Bde. H.Q. concerned.

3.   On completion of relief Nos 2 & 4 Sections will return to CARLISLE CAMP.

4.   Improvement of Emplacements will be carried out as quickly as possible by relieving Teams.

Copy No 1   2/Lt. PARSONS.
        2   2/Lt. WHEATLEY.
        3   2/Lt. DERBYSHIRE.
        4   2/Lt. ATTWATER.
        5   Office.
        6   War Diary.
        7   War Diary.

W.R. Thomson. Capt
O.C. 245 M.G. Coy.

Appendix 14.   **SECRET.**

Operation Order No 7 by Capt. W.R. Thomson
Commanding 245 M.G. Coy.
27th Sept. 1917.
Copy No 6

---

1. (a) On the night 30th Sept/1st Oct. 1917 No 4 Sect. will relieve No 1 Sect. in M.G. positions 50A, 51A, 52A (Right Sector) & 53A (Left Sector).

2/Lt. DERBYSHIRE will relieve 2/Lt. PARSONS in the ROOKERY.

(b) On the night 30th Sept/1st Oct. 1917 No 2 Sect. will relieve No 3 Sect. in M.G. positions 59 & 61 (3 guns) (Left Sector).

2/Lt. ATTWATER will relieve 2/Lt. WHEATLEY in RAKE TRENCH.

2. "Relief Complete" will be reported to Bde. H.Q. concerned.

3. On completion of relief Nos 1 & 3 Sects will return to CARLISLE CAMP.

4. In view of the relief of the Division in these Sectors by another Division at an early date every effort will be made to complete the improvements to emplacements so that they can be handed over in good condition for the future wet weather.

Copy No 1   2/Lt. DERBYSHIRE
       2   2/Lt. ATTWATER.
       3   2/Lt. PARSONS
       4   2/Lt. WHEATLEY.
       5   Office
       6   War Diary. ✓
       7   War Diary.

L R Thomson   Capt.
O.C. 245 M.G. Coy.

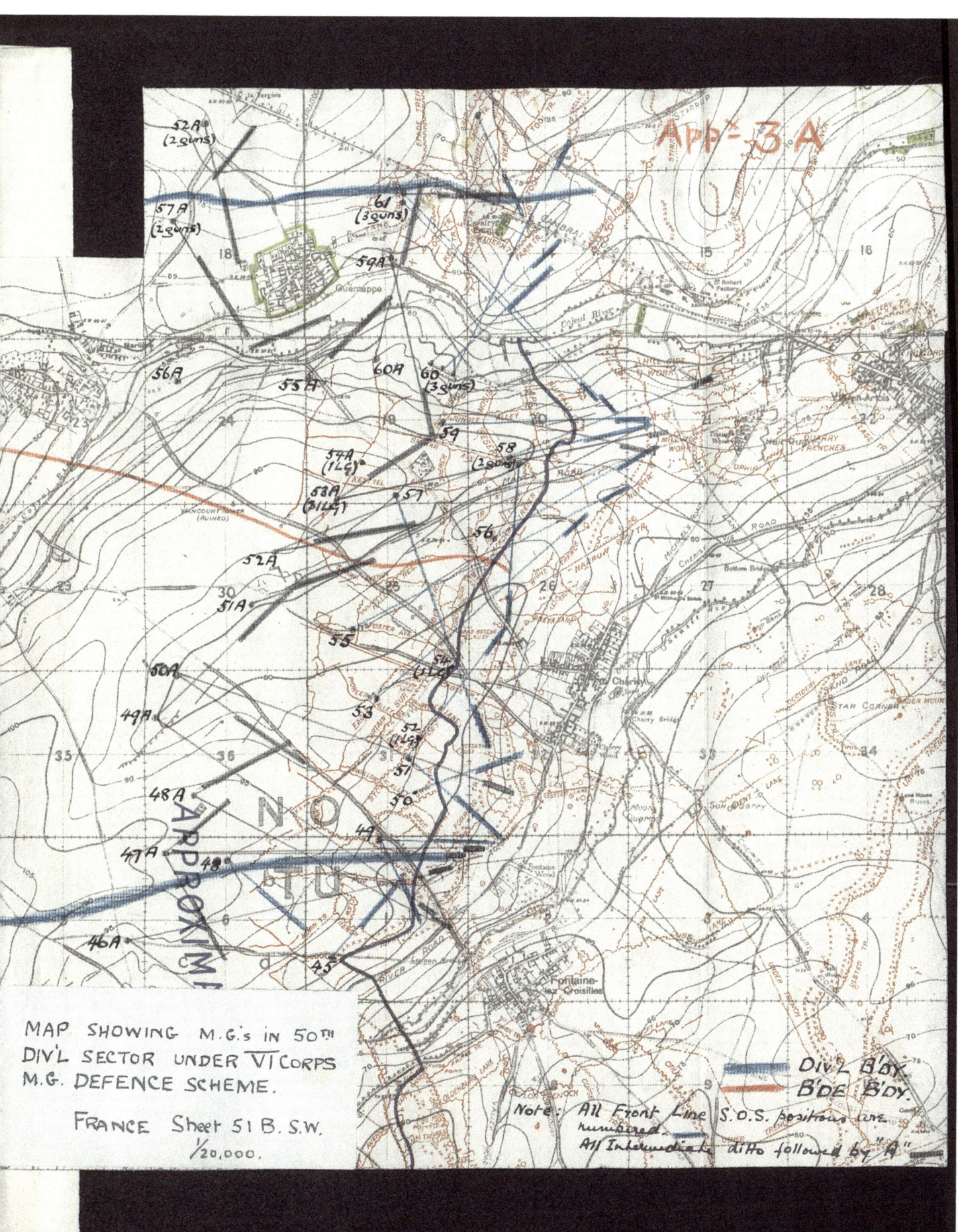

Vol 4

<u>CONFIDENTIAL</u>

<u>— WAR DIARY —</u>

— OF —

— <u>Nº 245 MACHINE GUN COMPANY</u>

<u>From 1ST OCT. To 31ST OCT. 1917.</u> —

<u>VOL III</u>   <u>ORIGINAL</u>

W R Thomson Capt.
O.C. 245 M.G. Coy.

Note: The WAR DIARY is numbered throughout in red.

Army Form C. 2118.

Page 1.

WAR DIARY
or
INTELLIGENCE SUMMARY
(Erase heading not required.)

Place	Date	Hour	Summary of Events and Information	Remarks and references to Appendices
CARLISLE CAMP Ref^{ce} 51B.S.W. 500x S. of BEAURAINS.	Oct. 1st		Received 50th Div. O.O. N° 127 - Coy to be relieved in CHERISY & VIS-EN-ARTOIS Sectors on 4th inst. Orders from Divⁿ to send Advance Party to ACHIET-LE-PETIT (M^p: LENS 11/100,000) to Training Ground. Arrive at Training Area on 2nd inst. Named Lt. A.V. BARNES for this duty. Received Div^l Administrative Instruction N° 16 regarding moves.	App. 1.
"	2nd.		Received G.H.Q. letter (via Divⁿ) 08/18·1 with orders that 1 complete MG Sectⁿ would be withdrawn of the Coy. Issued Lt. A.V. BARNES & 2/Lt. R.J. WHEATLEY that they would hold this Sectⁿ (N°3) in readiness to proceed overseas probably on 7th inst. Lt. BARNES proceeded with Advance Party to ACHIET-LE-PETIT. Received Amendment to O.O. N° 127 - Coy to be relieved by 232 MG Coy (51st Divⁿ. MG Coy) on 5th inst. & to proceed to ACHIET-LE-PETIT by march route on that day. N°3 Sectⁿ to entrain on 6th Oct. 17.	App. 2.
"	3rd		D.M.G.O. 51st Divⁿ & O.C. 232 MG Coy arrived to discuss details of relief. D.M.G.O. 50th Div. phoned orders to have N°3 Sectⁿ ready for inspection at 3 p.m. Sent orders to Lt. BARNES at ACHIET to return to Coy. DMGO inspected N° 3 Sectⁿ at 6 p.m. Lt. BARNES with his 12 men returned to Coy. O.O. N° 8 for relief of M.G.3 Sectⁿ & its by 232 MG Coy issued.	App. 3
"	4th.		DAPMG 50th Divⁿ inspected complete Sectⁿ for service overseas. Received orders for N° 3 Sectⁿ to proceed to ARRAS on 5th inst. to be billeted night 5/6th in ARRAS.	

WAR DIARY or INTELLIGENCE SUMMARY

Army Form C. 2118.

Place	Date	Hour	Summary of Events and Information	Remarks and references to Appendices
CARLISLE CAMP	4°		O.C. 232 M.G. Coy. arrived to take over Camp & Area Stores. Handed over everything & all particulars of 5th Corps M.G. Defence Scheme so far as 9th Section was concerned. Nos 2 & 4 Sectn. (8 guns) retained by Sectn. of 232 M.G. Coy. in positions 50A, 51A, 52A (Right Sector), 53A, 59A, 61 (38mm). (Left Sect.). Section returned Supply to camp. Sound Coy. O.O. No. 9 for march to ACHIET-LE-PETIT.	App. 4
	5°		Remainder of 232 M.G. Coy. arrived in Camp. 245 M.G. Coy. marched from Camp at 12.30 p.m. proceeding via ERVILLERS to ACHIET-LE-PETIT. arriving 4 p.m. No. 3 Sect. marched from CARLISLE CAMP to ARRAS at 4 p.m. Section Comprising:— LT. BARNES A.J. 2/LT. WHEATLEY R.J. 35 O.R. 4 T.G.'s Complete with equipment 3 Limbered G.S. waggons 10 mules (light draught). 1 Riding Horse. (Range finding Instrument was taken without trained Range finders). Accommodated in bivouac shelters in very muddy ground. Drew tents from AREA Conmdt. to accommodate all the Coy.	
ACHIET-LE-PETIT LENS 11 1/100,000	6°		Received circular letter 1073/115/ Central GHQ that boys from which Regt. has been withdrawn will be made up by reinforcements by A.G. & Q.M.G. Nucleus of new Sectn. to be found by a coy. furnishing men from previous drafts to their Regiments will be evenly distributed.	

Army Form C. 2118.

3

WAR DIARY
or
INTELLIGENCE SUMMARY.
(Erase heading not required.)

Place	Date	Hour	Summary of Events and Information	Remarks and references to Appendices
ACHIET-LE-PETIT.	7?		Week ending 13? Bn. to be devoted to intensive training. This became impossible owing to the persistently bad weather.	
"	10?		Rec'd 50? Div. G.952 Warning Order - 4 M.G.Coys.; 7? Div? to be prepared to move any time after midnight 10/11.? inst. Entraining St? BAPAUME. Rec'd G.954 - 4 M.G. Coys to entrain at ACHIET-LE-GRAND on 11? inst. Rec'd G.955 - G.954 cancelled.	
"	12?		Rec'd O.O. N? 128 - 50? Div? to entrain at BAPAUME & MIRAUMONT commencing 16? inst.	App. 5
"	13?		Advance Parties to report at 2-45 p.m. to DADRT ACHIET-LE-GRAND on 14? inst. 2 NCO's down to represent Coy.	
"	14? SAT.		Coy. took part in Assault Scheme carried out by 149 M.G. Inf. Bde. near COURCELLES, on same lines as known recent operations in North. Valuable lessons learnt by all concerned. Rec'd Bde. (150? Inf.) O.O. N? 127. M. making all information given in Div? O.O. N? 128. 245 M.G. Coy. attached to 150 Inf Bde for the move.	
"	15?		Rec'd S.C. 4986 (150 I.Bde.) O.O. N? 10 for entrainment. Move from 3rd Army to 5? Army. Train leaves 16-05 on 17? inst. via ARRAS & ST. POL. Detraining Station CASSEL.	App. 6

CASSEL
(HAZEBROUCK
5ᴬ Y.pres)

Army Form C. 2118.

WAR DIARY
or
INTELLIGENCE SUMMARY
(Erase heading not required.)

4

Place	Date	Hour	Summary of Events and Information	Remarks and references to Appendices
ACHIET-LE-PETIT.	17"	12 noon	Coy. marched from Camp to MIRAUMONT Sp.	
		12·30	Halted Camp over to AREA Commdt & obtained Clearance Certificate.	
		3 pm	Coy. completely entrained.	
		4·5	Train left MIRAUMONT arriving CASSEL 12·15 AM 18" inst.	
↓	18"		DAA&Q 50" Div. pointed out Coy's billets. Coy. marched from Sp. 2 AM arriving in billets at BROXEELE at 6 AM.	
BROXEELE Ref. HAZEBROUCK SA 1/100,000. & Sheet 1·27.			Recd. Dist. O.dr. No. 129 giving location of all units - 150 Tk. Eng. Bde., in RUBROUCK. Div. H.Q. at LEDERZEELE. Billets fairly comfortable - officers in empty house, men in barns. Billets v. very unsatisfactory owing only always a temporary billeting area for troops passing through.	
"	19"		Recd. Dist. Warning Order No. 130 Tk Bde. Warning Order (150 t Z Bde). to move on 21st inst. to PROVEN. Warned Coy. Recd. Dist. O.O. No. 131.	App. 7
"	20"		Saw B.M. 150 Bde. at RUBROUCK re move by own 2 arrangements for it. Lorries probably available. Recd. B.M. 3024 (150 t Z Bde) cancelling previous order re entraining Q move here Coy to ARNEKE Area on 21st inst. - commencing about 9 AM.	App. 8
	21st	6 AM	Recd. Bde. O.O. No. 128 & Amendment - No. 1 to 50" Div. O.O. No. 131 turned Coy. B.O. No. 11 for march to LA CLOCHE at 10 AM.	App. 9
LA CLOCHE Ref. HAZEBROUCK SP 1/100,000		10 AM	Coy. marched from BROXEELE to LA CLOCHE via "les 5 Rues" arriving at billets LA CLOCHE at 1 pm. St. REES conducted Coy. to billets. Very comfortable.	App. 10
		4 pm	Recd. O.O. No. 129 (150 t Z Bde.) for move tomorrow. General Coy. B.O. No. 12 for march to PROVEN tomorrow.	App. 11

WAR DIARY
INTELLIGENCE SUMMARY

Army Form C. 2118.

Place	Date	Hour	Summary of Events and Information	Remarks and references to Appendices
LA CLOCHE	22	1 A.M.	Raid taken from 150 I.Bde. to PROVEN. This being practically all the marching troops and CAPT. HOUGHTON Half-Co would conduct the troops from the air & have Coy. column on reaching WORMHOUDT.	
"		8 A.M.	Marched from billets passing starting point WORMHOUDT Square at 10.42 A.M. To have B & C Coys during of our Column to entrain. Remainder (L. Transport) proceeded by road via HOUTKERQUE to PROVEN (midday meal E. of HOUTKERQUE). Arrived at POMPEY CAMP, PROVEN, at 3.30 p.m. Motor-lorry carrying host of stores (C.Q.M.S. & blankets). Rec'd SD² Div² D.O. N° 132. x Amendments to Same.	App. 12
PROVEN (Ref⁴ HAZEBROUCK SA 1/100,000 F Sheet 27).	23		Attended Conference with D.M.G.O. at Div⁴ H.Q. PROVEN at 5 p.m. All M.G's of 24ᵗʰ M.G.Coy would be going in on night 25/26? war-- Rec'd Coy. O.O. N° 13	App. 13
"	24		Received wire O.C. 150 M.G.Coy to SIGNAL FM (M.G.Coy H.Q in M°Luis) to reconnoitre ground. Retaining 106 M.G.Coy. — this Coy (Recond) Stated he was to withdraw his gun from PASCAL FM at 8 p.m. 24ᵗʰ inst if no relief appeared. Guns of this Coy not ready to come in until? tomorrow. Rec'd 50ᵗʰ Div² O.O. N° 133 and Appendix 3. INCO 824 Rein attached to Coy on arrival from 151ˢᵗ Inf. Bde.	App. 14
FRIEDLAND FARM 28 N.W. 20,000 B.25.d.8.2	25		Issued Coy. O.O. N° 14. Capt. HOUGHTON × 2/Lt PARSONS took 11 guns to PASCAL FM (See map) to give barrage fire during attack. Coy. H.Q. moved to SIGNAL FM (2/Lt. DERBYSHIRE 2/Lt. Coy. H.Q.) Guns were in position at 10 p.m. Received hand from Capt Houghton at 11 p.m x Lieut "ARRAS" to H.Q. 169ᵗʰ Inf. Bde. Raid barrage Lieut DIv² H.Q. (through Transport) Zero was to be 5.40 A.M. Sent M.M. to Capt HOUGHTON.	App. 15

WAR DIARY or INTELLIGENCE SUMMARY

Army Form C. 2118.

Place	Date	Hour	Summary of Events and Information	Remarks and references to Appendices
VAL F^m SW.4 40,000	26°	5-40 AM	149° Inf. Bde attacked on Brit^t front. Right of Railway completely held up by Concrete huts & huts in VIA (SCHAAP BALIE 40,000) heavy MG fire from this point caused heavy casualties. No casualties amongst gunners in shell holes at PASCAL F^m — positions chosen were just beyond German first Barrage but though heavy stray shots fell near. Communication between SIGNAL & PASCAL F^{ms} was maintained throughout. Saw B.M. 149° Inf. Bde at MARTIN'S MILL. Attack failed. My MG's to remain until D.M.G.O. cams. Received SD. DIV. N° 182. FRIEDLAND F^m bombed by E.A.	App. 16
"	27°		D.M.G.O. arrived and gave orders for all my guns to withdraw from PASCAL F^m on 27° night. Issued Coy. O.O. N° 15. Capt HOUGHTON, 2/LT. PARSONS with 7 guns withdrew via HUNTER S? to FRIEDLAND F^m. 2/LT. DERBYSHIRE remained at SIGNAL F^m with 4 guns and 3 men /team. Coy. H.Q. moved from SIGNAL to FRIEDLAND F^m (Transport Lines). Rec^d SD° Divⁿ W.O. N° 134 & SD° Divⁿ O.O. N° 135. Casualties for 1st battle — 2 attached infantry wounded. FRIEDLAND F^m bombed by E.A.	App. 17 App. 18
FRIEDLAND F^m	"	3 p.m.		
"	28°		Hun's Coy from Business Station moving to surrounding and into huts on fresh dugout ground. Built sandbag walls round every door. Issued orders that during bombing raid no man was to leave his hut. Casualties always occur if men stand up outside.	

WAR DIARY
or
INTELLIGENCE SUMMARY

Army Form C. 2118.

Place	Date	Hour	Summary of Events and Information	Remarks and references to Appendices
FRIEDLAND F^m	29th		Rec^d 50th Divⁿ W.O. N°136. D.M.G.O. gave in particulars of minor operation to be carried out on night 30/31st Oct. by 150th Inf. Bde. 2/Lt. Derbyshire & gun Coo to PASCAL F^m	App. 19
"	30th		Rec^d 50th Divⁿ O.O. N°138 & 150th I. Bde. O.O. N°133 for minor o/peration. Issued Coy. O.O. N° 16 to 7/Pt. Derbyshire who received detailed orders for the battle from B.G.C. 150th Inf. Bde. Rec^d 50th Divⁿ O.O. N°139 for Infantry Relief. 2/Lt. Derbyshire with 4 guns moves from SIGNAL to PASCAL F^m to be in posⁿ. for battle by 12 midnight.	App. 20 App. 21
"		9 p.m.		
"	31st		Operation unsuccessful owing to detection of movement in moonlight by enemy & consequent heavy enemy M.G. fire. Saw B.G.C. 150th I. Bde. at PASCAL MARTIN'S MILL & obtained permission to withdraw 2/Lt. DERBYSHIRE with 4 guns from PASCAL F^m after moving to 31 post 1st Nov. Sent orders to 1/Lt. DERBYSHIRE that to send & withdraw his guns to SIGNAL F^m & bring his men back to FRIEDLAND F^m— men to commence at midnight. Enemy Artillery very active over whole Sector. ELVERDINGHE Area bombed heavily by E.A. from 6.30 p.m. to 2 A.m.	

W R Thomson Capt.
O.C. 245 M.G. Coy.

LIST OF APPENDICES TO ACCOMPANY THE
WAR DIARY

Sheet 8

of 245 Machine Gun Company for Month of OCTOBER 1917.

Appendix No	Subject, Date of Issue, Author etc.
1	50th Divn. O.O. No 127 1st Oct. 17. 1. 50th Divn (less Artillery) to be relieved by 51st Divn (less Artillery) between 4th & 6th Oct. 17. 2. Divn to be accommodated in GOMIECOURT – COURCELLES – ACHIET-LE-PETIT Area 3. 245 M.G. Coy. to be relieved by 232 MG Coy on 4th Oct. & to proceed to ACHIET-LE-PETIT. (amended later to 5th Oct.) G.S. 50th Divn
2	G.H.Q. Letter OB/181 Withdrawal of Sectn from Coy. (attached)
3	Coy. O.O. No 8 for March Relief of Guns in line by 232 MG Coy. (attached)
4	Coy. O.O. No 9 for March to ACHIET. (attached)
5	50th Divn. O.O. No 128 12th Oct. 17. 1. 50th Divn to commence entraining at BAPAUME & MIRAUMONT on 16th inst. 2. 245 MG Coy in 150th Inf Bde Group for Move. 3. Coy. to entrain in 6th train from MIRAUMONT. G.S. 50th Divn
6	Coy. O.O. No 10 for Entrainment of Coy. (attached).
7	50th Divn. O.O. No 131. 19th Oct. 17. 1. 50th Divn (less Artillery) to be transferred from II to XIV Corps & to move from ZEGGERS-CAPPEL Area to PROVEN Central Area on Oct. 20th, 21st, 22nd. 2. Artillery to move direct to XIV Corps area by rail. 3. 245 MG Coy in 150 Inf Bde Group to move from RUBROUCK Area to PROVEN on Oct. 21st by road. G.S. 50th Divn
8	150th Inf Bde. B.M. 3024 & Amendment No 1 to 50th Divn. O.O. No 131 20th Oct. 1917 1. 150th I. Bde. Group to move to ARNEKE Area on 21st inst. by march route in Relief of 151st I. Bde. 2. Move to commence about 9 A.M. 150th Inf. Bde. O.O. No 128 21st Oct. 17. 1. 245 M.G. Coy to move to billets at LA CLOCHE via LES 5 RUES at 10 A.M. 21st inst. Brigade Major 150 Inf. Bde.
9	Coy. O.O. No 11 for march to LA CLOCHE (attached)
10	150th Inf. Bde O.O. No 129 21st Oct. 17. 1. Group to move to PROVEN No 1 Area on 22nd inst. 2. 1 Lorry for 245 MG Coy to carry packs &c. 3. 245 MG Coy to pass WORMHOUDT Central at 10-42 A.M. Brigade Major 150 Inf Bde.

LIST OF APPENDICES (CONT'D).   Sheet 9

245 M.G. Coy.

Appendix Nº	Subject, Date of Issue, Author &c.
11	Coy. O.O. Nº 12 for march to PROVEN. (attached).
12	50ᵗʰ Divⁿ O.O. Nº 132 & Amendments & Additions 22ⁿᵈ Oct. 17. 1. 50ᵗʰ Divⁿ to relieve a portion of 34ᵗʰ Divⁿ in the line. Relief to commence on Oct. 23ʳᵈ to complete by 8 AM 25ᵗʰ Oct. 2. Divⁿ H.Q. ELVERDINGHE CHÂᵤ 149ᵗʰ Inf Bde - In Line, 150ᵗʰ Inf Bde - In Support, 151ˢᵗ Inf Bde in Corps Staging Area (ST SIXTE). 3. 245 MG Coy. to move from PROVEN P1 AREA to FRIEDLAND Fᵐ B23.d.8.2 (BELGIUM Sheet 28 NW) on 24ᵗʰ inst. G.S. 50ᵗʰ Divⁿ
13	Coy. O.O. Nº 13 for move to FRIEDLAND Fᵐ (attached)

14	50ᵗʰ Divⁿ O.O. Nº 133 24ᵗʰ Oct. 1917
	 1. XIV Corps in conjunction with XVIII Corps on Right & 1ˢᵗ French Army on left will attack & capture the blue line on attached Map (Appˣ 14 A) on 26ᵗʰ inst. Zero hour to be notified later.
	 2. 50ᵗʰ Divⁿ objective from STADENDREVEBEKE (inclusive) to crosstracks at U.6.b.95.40.
	 3. Assault to be carried out by 149ᵗʰ Inf. Bde.
	 4. Attack to be made under (C) M.G. Barrage.
	 5. 245 MG Coy to provide 12 guns for Barrage in accordance with Appendix 14 A (Map - posⁿˢ & targets shown).
	 6. S.O.S. Signal 5ᵗʰ Army Front - 2 Red & 2 Green.
	 Appendix Nº 3 to above O.O. 24ᵗʰ Oct. 17.
	 M.G. Barrage. 245 MG Coy 12 guns.
	 Fire in 3 phases (a) 1ˢᵗ Zero to Z + 6 mins
	                    (b) 2ⁿᵈ Z+14 to Z+20
	                    (c) 3ʳᵈ Z+40 to Z+ 3 hrs
	 Rate of fire: 1 belt / 6 mins.
	 If S.O.S. Signal given guns will fire on S.O.S. Targets laid down for 3ʳᵈ Phase for 10 mins. at rate of 1 belt / 2 mins.
	                     G.S. 50ᵗʰ Divⁿ

15	Coy. O.O. Nº 14 for 1ˢᵗ Battle (attached).
16	50ᵗʰ Divⁿ G 182 (O.O.) 26ᵗʰ Oct. 17. 1. 150ᵗʰ Inf. Bde to relieve 149ᵗʰ Inf Bde in line G.S. 50ᵗʰ Divⁿ
17	Coy. O.O. Nº 15 for withdrawal of guns 27ᵗʰ Oct. 17. (attached)
18	50ᵗʰ Divⁿ O.O. Nº 135 26ᵗʰ Oct. 17. 149ᵗʰ Inf. Bde in Divⁿ Reserve 151 Inf Bde in Support (150ᵗʰ Inf Bde in line). G.S. 50ᵗʰ Divⁿ
19	50ᵗʰ Divⁿ W.O. Nº 136 29ᵗʰ Oct. 17. 1. XIV Corps H.Q. has been relieved by XIX Corps HQ 2. XIX Corps will resume the attack on "Wa" Day in co-operation with XVIII Corps on right & 1ˢᵗ French Army on left - 57ᵗʰ 50ᵗʰ 35ᵗʰ Divⁿˢ. 3. Objectives as shown on map Appendix 14 A. 151ˢᵗ I. Bde to attack. 245 M.G. Coy will co-operate in Barrage work. G.S. 50ᵗʰ Divⁿ

LIST OF APPENDICES (CONT'D)   Sheet 10

245 M.G. Coy.

Appendix No	Subject. Date of Issue, Author &c.
20	50° Div: O.O. No 138 & 150° I. Bde O.O. No 133 29° Oct 17. 1. A minor operation will be carried out by 150° Inf. Bde. on night 30/31st Oct. 17. 2. Line to be advanced from pos: marked to a pos: marked (Refer Map App: 14A). 3. A heavy protective artillery barrage has been arranged when called for by S.O.S. Signal. 4. 4 guns 245 MG Coy. are to be laid on S.O.S. barrage lines - only to be fired when S.O.S. signal given. 5. Troops to be in pos: by 12 M.N. 30/31st Oct. [Zero received later - 2 A.M. 31st Oct.] G.S. 50° Div" & B.M. 150° I. Bde.
21	Coy. O.O. No 16. for Battle (attached)

List of Appendices is followed by copies of actual appendices marked above as (attached)

L.R. Thomson Capt:
O.C. 245 M.G. Coy.

Appendix 2

11

SECRET.

OB/181   **I**   Third Army G 26/279

Under instructions rec'd from Home Authorities certain Sect'ns will be withdrawn from M.G. Coy's & held in readiness to proceed overseas by 6th Oct. 17.

1 Sect: (4 guns) from 1 MG Coy. of each of :-
12th, 15th, 24th, 34th, 35th, 40th, 50th, 51st, 55th & 62nd Div'ns
& 1 Sect: from 2 MG Coy's of each of :-
     20th & 56th Div'ns

Adv. GHQ   (Sgd) K. WIGRAM B.G. for L.G.
29.9.17.   C.G.S.

245 M.G. Coy.   **II**   50th Div'n GX 4601/1 XC.

1 Sect: of 245 M.G. Coy will be held in readiness

2nd.10.17.   (Sgd) E.C. ANSTEY Lt. Col.
     G.S. 50th Div'n

H.Q. 50th Div'n   **III**   TY 9/3.

Names of Officers   LT. BARNES A.J
     2/LT. WHEATLEY R.J.

Personnel
    2 Officers   1 Riding Horse
    2 Sergts
    2 Corpls
    24 Privates   4 M.G.'s
    5 Drivers   10 Mules
    2 Batmen   3 G.S. Limb'd Wag?
    37 TOTAL

2.10.17.   W.R. Thomson Capt.
     O.C. 245 M.G. Coy.

245 M.G. Coy.   **IV**   50th Div'n Q 173.

Sect: will leave ARRAS for MARSEILLES at 16-36 hours tomorrow (6th inst.)

5th Oct. 17.   50th Div'n Q.

(2 Copies for War Diary)

     W.R. Thomson Capt.
10th Oct. 17.   O.C. 245 M.G. Coy.

SECRET.

Operation Order No. 8 by Capt. W. R. Thomson
Commanding 245 M.G. Coy.
3rd Oct. 1917.
Copy No. 3

---

1. (a) On the night 4/5th Oct. 1917 4 teams of No. 232 M.G. Coy. will relieve No. 4 Sect. in 50A, 51A, 52A (Right Sector) & 53A (Left Sector).

   2/Lt. DERBYSHIRE will return with No. 4 Sect. to CARLISLE CAMP on completion of relief.

   (b) On the night 4/5th Oct. 1917 4 teams of No. 232 M.G. Coy. will relieve No. 2 Sect. in 59A & 61 (3 guns) (Left Sector).

   LT. HOUGHTON & 2/LT. ATTWATER will return with No. 2 Sect. to CARLISLE CAMP on completion of relief.

2. No. 1's will remain with the relieving teams until 10 A.M. 5th Oct. when they will return to CAMP.

3. All Trench Maps 1/20,000 & 1/10,000 will be handed over to the relieving Officers & receipts obtained.

4. Receipts to be obtained for S.A.A. tools handed over.

5. Limbers will wait at FOSTER DUMP No. 4 Sect. & RAKE DUMP for No. 2 Sect.

6. Time of relief will be about 12 Midnight.

7. The telephone instruments will be disconnected & brought down by 2/LT. DERBYSHIRE. The wire will be handed over & receipt obtained.

8. Officers & O.R. will give every assistance to the relieving Sections.

W. R. Thomson Capt.
O.C. 245 M.G. Coy.

3rd Oct. 1917.

Copies to: 1. 2/LT. DERBYSHIRE
2. LT. HOUGHTON
3. 232 M.G. Coy. ✓
4. Office
5. 6. War Diary.

SECRET.   13

Operation Order No 9 by Capt. W.R. Thomson   App^x 4.
            Commndg 245 M.G. Coy.
LENS 11 1/100,000.   4th Oct. 1917.

1.   The Coy. on completion of relief by 232
M.G. Coy will move by march route to training
Area at ACHIET-LE-PETIT tomorrow 5th inst.

2.   The portion of CARLISLE CAMP occupied
by this Coy will be handed over to the relieving
Coy & receipts for all Stores obtained.

3.   Parade to move off at 12.15 p.m.
facing South on Main Road opposite Camp.

4.   Route — MERCATEL, BOIRY-BECQUERRELLES,
ERVILLERS, GOMIECOURT, ACHIET-LE-GRAND, ACHIET-LE-
PETIT.

5.   The time spent at the Training Area
will be devoted to Intensive Training according
to programme laid-down.

Issued at 5 p.m.   W R Thomson Capt.
4. Oct. 17.   O.C. 245 M.G. Coy.

SECRET.   14

Operation Order No. 10 by Capt. W R Thomson
Commandig 245 M.G. Coy.   App: 6.

LENS 11 } 1/100,000.   15? Oct. 17.
HAZEBROUCK 5A

1. The Coy. will entrain at MIRAUMONT Station at 3 p.m. 17? inst. Coy. will parade to leave Camp at ACHIET-LE-PETIT at 12 noon 17? inst.

2. Transport will accompany column but vehicles will be loaded and unloaded by a special loading party from 151 Inf. Bde. Animals will be entrained by own parties.

3. The Camp will be left clean and handed over to the AREA COMMANDANT at 12.30 p.m. A certificate of Cleanliness will be obtained.

4. An Advance Party of 2 NCO's to take over billets has gone forward and will meet the Coy. at the detraining point to conduct them to billeting Area.

5. Train leaves MIRAUMONT 4·5 p.m. Detraining St?: CASSEL (Refd HAZEBROUCK 5A) via ARRAS & ST. POL. Probably arrive about 1 A.M. 18? inst.

Issued at 10 A.M.   W R Thomson Capt?
15? Oct. 17   O.C. 245 M.G. Coy.

SECRET.

App: 9

Operation Order No 11 by Capt W R Thomson
    Commdg 245 M.G. Coy.
HAZEBROUCK 5A. 1/100,000   21st Oct. 1917.
_____

1.   The Coy. will move by march route to LA CLOCHE today 21.10.17. passing Starting Point (Coy HQ.) at 10 A.M.
         Route - LES 5 RUES - LA CLOCHE.

2.   Lieut. L.W. REES with 2 cyclist orderlies will proceed via RUBROUCK to LA CLOCHE as Advance Billeting Party. A guide from this party will be at the entrance of village (from direction of LES 5 RUES) at 11.45 A.M. to conduct the column to billets. Staff Captain 150 I. Bde. will be at ARNEKE from 9 AM onwards.

3.   The Coy. will be moving by march route on 22nd inst. to PROVEN starting at about 7 A.M.

Issued at 7-40 A.M.   W R Thomson Capt.
21st Oct. 17.   O.T. 245 MG Coy.

SECRET

16

App. 11

Operation Order No 12 by Capt. W.R.Thomson
Commdg 245 M.G. Coy.

HAZEBROUCK 5A/100,000.   21st Oct. 1917.

_____

1.   The Coy. will move by march route to the PROVEN No 1 AREA on 22nd inst with the 150th Inf Bde.

2.   Move off from Coy H.Q. 8.0 A.M. to pass Starting Point (WORMHOUDT Central) at 10.42 A.M.

3.   Breakfasts 6.30 A.M. Halt for dinners (Haversack Rations) will be made at 10.50 AM. March will be resumed at 12.30 p.m.

4.   Packs, blankets & 2.M. Stores will be carried on a lorry. Packs to be at Coy H.Q. at 6 A.M.
   1 Signaller will be detailed by Corpl. MITCHELL to be at Bde H.Q. ARNEKE at 6.30 AM to guide lorry to Coy. H.Q.

5.   Lt. L.W. REES & 2 Signallers (with cycles) as Advance Party will report to Staff Capt. 150 Inf Bde at AREA COMMDT'S OFFICE, PROVEN at 10.30 A.M. The Column will probably arrive in PROVEN at 3.30 p.m.

6.   Route :- ERINGHEM, LA CLOCHE, ESQUELBECQ, WORMHOUDT, HERZEELE, HOUTKERQUE, PROVEN   (14 miles).

7.   Dress :- Fighting Order. Steel Helmets to be worn.

8.   West of POPERINGHE - PROVEN Road 500" will be maintained between Units, & Units & their Transport. East of same this distance will be 200".

Issued at 9.25 p.m.   W.R.Thomson Capt.
21st Oct. 17.   O.C. 245 M.G. Coy.

SECRET.

Appx 13.

Operation Order No 13 by Capt. W R Thomson
              Commdg 245 M.G. Coy.
HAZEBROUCK 5A 1/100,000   23rd Oct. 1917.
BELGIUM 28 NW 1/20,000.

1.   The Coy. will move to FRIEDLAND FARM B.23.b.8.2 (BELGIUM 28 N.W.) tomorrow 24? inst.

(a)   Personnel will entrain at PROVEN Stn at 9 AM & detrain at ELVERDINGHE St. marching by direct route to FRIEDLAND via DAWSON'S CORNER.

(b)   The Transport will move by road from PROVEN to FRIEDLAND Fm at 8.30 AM by route issued to the Transport officer. Head of column to pass Starting Point (X-Rds ½ mile N.W. of PROVEN) at 9.20 A.M.

2.   On arrival at FRIEDLAND Fm Horse Lines will be prepared and bivouacs and Shelters taken over for the men.

3.   All Shelters will be surrounded by a sandbag wall 3 ft. high for defence against bomb splinters.

4.   The Signal for approach of E.A. will be 3 Short whistle-blasts.

Issued at 10.35 p.m.   W R Thomson Capt.
23rd Oct. 1917.   O.C. 245 M.G. Coy.

18

App.^x 15

SECRET.

Operation Order No 14 by Capt W R Thomson
Commd^g 245 M.G. Coy.

20 S.W. 4 1/10,000   25th Oct. 1917.
SCHAAP-BALIE 1/10,000

1/ The 50th Divⁿ will attack & capture a final objective running through U.6.b.9.4. COLBERT-X-RDS, V 2 d 1.5., on 26th inst at a ZERO hour to be given later.

2/ 11 Guns of 245 M.G. Coy. will proceed from FRIEDLAND F^m at 12 noon today to positions to be selected and improved at U.12.C.40.55. via HUNTER ST. Guns on pack animals will proceed by road to the junction of HUNTER ST with the WIJDENDRIFT-LANGEMARCK Road. From that point guns & tripods will be carried to PASCAL F^m.

3/ Capt. J.R. HOUGHTON will be in command of the 11 guns. 1 LT. H.M. PARSONS will assist him. 1 Sgt 1 Cpl & No^s 1 & 5 of each team only will remain at PASCAL F^m. The remaining personnel will return to Transport. 1 Sgt & 24 men have been attached to the Coy. as carriers. Capt HOUGHTON will make use of these as he likes.

4/ Coy. H.Q. at SIGNAL F^m. U22.C.0.7. Sect. H.Q. will be at PASCAL F^m. Bde H.Q. at MARTIN'S MILL. U22 C.3.6.

5/ Orderlies will be as follows:
6 orderlies at PASCAL F^m   Sect: HQ
6   "   " SIGNAL F^m   Coy. HQ
2   "   " MARTIN'S MILL.   Bde. HQ
2   "   " FRIEDLAND F^m   Transport
2   "   " ELVERDINGHE CH^{au}   Div^l HQ.

6/ Capt. HOUGHTON will report to Coy H.Q. when guns are ready to fire so that code word "ARRAS" may be sent from Coy H.Q. to Bde H.Q.

7/ Rations for 2 days will be carried by all ranks at & beyond Coy. H.Q.
2 Tins clean water per team will be carried.
There are sufficient belt boxes at PASCAL F^m for 11 guns.
SAA. dump at VEE BEND.

8/ Firing programme attached.

Issued at 9 A.M.   W R Thomson Capt:
25th Oct. 1917.   O.C. 245 M.G. Coy

SECRET.

App. 15A.

Appendix No 1 to Coy O.O. No 14
Ref. SCHAAP-BALIE 1/10,000.   25? Oct. 1917.

Programme of M.G. Fire.

1.   11 Guns in 3 Groups D, E & F.
Targets :- D Group   SIX ROADS V.1.b.7.7. for 1st
                     & 2nd phases.
                     P.32.C 15 25 for 3rd phase.
           E Group   KLEBER X. RDS P31d 60 15
           F Group   Level Crossing P31d 50. 60.

2.   Guns will be found as follows
No 2 Sect: 4 guns   D Group
No 1 Sect: 3 guns   E "
No 4 Sect: 4 guns   F "

3.   Rates of fire will be :-
1st Phase   Zero to Zero + 6 mins   1 belt / 6 mins
2nd "   Zero + 14 to Z. + 20 mins   "
3rd "   Zero + 40 to Z + 3 hrs   1 belt / min
             with ½ guns firing alternately

4.   In the event of
   (a) S.O.S. (2 red & 2 green) being sent up or
   (b) The counter-attack aeroplane dropping
       a smoke bomb breaking 100 ft. from ground
       into a white parachute light descending
       slowly & leaving a broad trail of brown
       smoke behind it,
                                  rapid fire at 1 belt/min
will be immediately given on S.O.S. lines
(targets as given above) for 10 mins.

Issued with O.O. No 14   W R Thomson Capt:
25? Oct. 17.   O.C. 245 MG Coy.

Appendix 14 A.

MAP OF BATTLE

to

accompany Coy. O.O. Nº 15

and Coy. O.O. Nº 16.

Scale 1/20,000.
[A portion of BELGIUM 20 SW
& S.E.]

For WAR DIARY
245 M.G. Coy.

Appendix 14 A

O13 – D15

TRENCH MAP
1/20,000.

MAP OF BATTLE
to
accompany Coy. O.O. Nº 15
and Coy. O.O. Nº 16.

Scale 1/20,000.
[A portion of BELGIUM 20 SW
& S.E.]

For WAR DIARY
245 M.G. Coy.

SECRET.

App: 7

Operation Order No 15 by Capt W R Thomson
                Commdg 245 M. G. Coy.

SCHAAP-BALIE 1/10,000.   27° Oct. 1917.

1.   All guns of this Coy. at PASCAL FM with the exception of those given in Para 2 will be withdrawn to Camp tonight.
        Pack animals will be at the junction of HUNTER ST with the WIJDENDRIFT-LANGEMARCK road at 3 p.m. today 27° inst.
        3 Limbers will be in BOESINGHE where HUNTER ST ends on the main road at 5 p.m.

2.   No 4 Sect. with guns will withdraw immediately on receipt of this order to Coy. H.Q. at SIGNAL FM where 3 men per team 1 Sgt & 1 Cpl will be accommodated in reserve. 2/Lt. DERBYSHIRE will remain with this Sect.

3.   Coy. H.Q. will close at SIGNAL FM and open again at FRIEDLAND FM at 6 p.m.

Issued at 9.30 AM   W R Thomson Capt.
27° Oct. 1917.   O.C. 245 MG Coy.

SECRET.

App 21.

Operation Order No 16 by Capt. W R Thomson
Commdg 245 M.G. Coy.

SCHAAP-BALIE 1/10,000   30th Oct. 1917.

1.   A minor operation will be carried out by 150 Inf Bde (4th E. Yorks) on night 30/31st Oct. to advance our line on the left of the Railway. A blue line COLOMBO Ho V.1.a.00.35., V.1.a.7.2, V1 central, TURENNE CROSSING will be consolidated.

2.   Zero hour will be notified later - the code word "ADEN" will be used.

3.   4 M.G's under 2/Lt. DERBYSHIRE will move forward from SIGNAL Fm to Positions at PASCAL Fm on the night 30/31st. Targets for these guns will be given to 2/Lt. DERBYSHIRE by 150 Inf. Bde. These guns will only fire on the S.O.S. call being made.

4.   2/Lt. DERBYSHIRE will withdraw his Sectn less 2 men to Camp at dawn on 2nd Nov. The 4 M.G's will be left at PASCAL Fm to be handed over by the 2 men to a Sectn of this Coy. that will arrive on the night of 2nd/3rd Nov.

5.   Communication will be made between PASCAL Fm and EGYPT Ho (Battn HQ) and to MARTIN'S MILL (Bde HQ).
     Coy. H.Q. at FRIEDLAND Fm.

Issued at 8 A.M   W R Thomson Capt.
30th Oct. 1917.   O.C. 245 M.G. Coy.

Note:- Zero hour 2 A.M. 31st Oct. notified by 150th Inf Bde direct to 2/Lt DERBYSHIRE.

CONFIDENTIAL

Vol 5

WAR DIARY

OF

245 MACHINE GUN COMPANY

from

1st Nov. 1917 to 30th Nov. 1917.

Volume IV

ORIGINAL COPY.

(1st Dec. 1917.)

W R Thomson Capt:
O.C. 245 M.G. Coy.

WAR DIARY
or
INTELLIGENCE SUMMARY.

Army Form C. 2118.

Sheet 1.

Place	Date	Hour	Summary of Events and Information	Remarks and references to Appendices
FRIEDLAND FARM B.23.b.8.2. Sheet 28.	Nov 1		Coy. distributed as follows - Midnight 31st Oct/1st Nov. Coy. H.Q. - FRIEDLAND FARM in Bivouac Shelters & tents. Transport - do. 2 Sections do. 1 Section under 2/Lt. DERBYSHIRE moving back to Camp from PASCAL FM where he had been in position for barrage fire for a minor operation by 150" Inf Bde on night 30/31st Oct. left at- SIGNAL FM with 2 men. Remainder after very heavy journey (Gas Shells & H.E.) reached Camp safely at 4 A.M. Owing to non. success of 150" I. Bde. operation the Bn. operation that was to take place about 5th inst. has been indefinitely postponed. Received 50th Divn. Order No 140 D.M.G.O. first drew our guns to be withdrawn from SIGNAL FM back to Camp & that the Coy. would turn to the ST. SIXTE Area tomorrow. 2nd inst - sent a carrying party to SIGNAL FM for the 4 guns & carried the Coy of the tents. Received detailed orders for move from D.M.G.O. repeated them in Coy. O.O. 19.	App. 1. App. 2.
do.	2		Div. authorized our using a Motor lorry for the move. Handed over FRIEDLAND FM Camp to the Camp Warden. Coy. marched from Camp at 2/3 p.m. via ELVERDINGHE arriving at SUTTON CAMP at 5-30 p.m. Plenty of accommodation in and	
SUTTON CAMP F.10.b.6.5. Sheet 27				

WAR DIARY
or
INTELLIGENCE SUMMARY.

(Erase heading not required.)

Army Form C. 2118.

Sheet 2.

Place	Date	Hour	Summary of Events and Information	Remarks and references to Appendices
SUTTON CAMP F.10.b.6.5. Sheet 27.	2nd		Rec'd 50º Div'n Order Nº 141 - 50º Div'n to partake in no further operations and to be relieved by 10º inst.	App x 3
	3rd		Issued Addendum Nº 1 to 50º Div'n Order Nº 141 (see App x 3)	
	5th		Issued 50º Div'n Order Nº 142 for later Brigade Relief's & movements.	App x 4
	8th		Rec'd 50º Div'n Order Nº 143 for move of Div'n to back area EPERLECQUES - #1 repeated in 150º Inf Bde Order Nº 136 of 9º inst. 245 MG Coy moves with this Bde.	
	9th		Rec'd 150º Inf Bde O.O. Nº 135 50º Div'n relieved in the line by 12th Div'n in night 9/10º inst. Issued O.O. Nº 20.	App x 5 App x 6
	10th		LT. REES with 2 Signallers proceeded on Advance Party to HELLEBROUCQ Issued O.O. Addendum Nº 1 to O.O. Nº 20.	App x 7

Army Form C. 2118.

Sheet 3.

WAR DIARY
or
INTELLIGENCE SUMMARY.

(Erase heading not required.)

Place	Date	Hour	Summary of Events and Information	Remarks and references to Appendices
SUTTON CAMP	10th		Transport of Coy. left CAMP at 7.45 A.M. joining Brigade Column (150?) at PROVEN. Proceeded by road to BUYSSCHEURE. Weather very wet.	
do.	11th		Left SUTTON CAMP at 10.30 A.M. marching to INTERNATIONAL CORNER (Sheet 28 N.W. Belgium) Entrained 11.15 A.M. Train left 11-30 A.M. Arrived WATTEN (HAZEBROUCK 5A 1/100,000 & FRANCE 27A N.E. 1/20,000) 4.30 P.M. Met Lt. REES who conducted Coy. to billets at HELLEBROUCQ. Arrived in billets 6 P.M. Very comfortable & plenty of accommodation. Coy H.Q. in CHATEAU.	
HELLEBROUCQ 5A 1/100,000 & 27A 1/20,000.	12th		Made out Programme of Training for week ending 17? Nov. Elementary Training, Rifle Range Work and Route march. During period of rest non-attention to A.S. to be paid to Recreational training. In his own some the 50? Div. has many and competition in football, boxing wrestling & running. The men show keenness in entering & having interesting competition in the Company were held on 17? 19? 20? & 21st Nov. The Coy. is included under Div. H.Q. which counts in the whole competitions as a Brigade. 1 man was selected from the Coy. for the Div. H.Q. 700 Ball Team.	

Army Form C. 2118.

Sheet-4.

WAR DIARY
or
INTELLIGENCE SUMMARY.

(Erase heading not required.)

Place	Date	Hour	Summary of Events and Information	Remarks and references to Appendices
HELEBROUCQ	23-		The Coy. took part in a Tactical Scheme in the Training Area. W.op EPERLECQUES. The 150th Inf Bde conducted an attack upon the enemy positions held by the 73rd NFs and 245 M.G. Coy. Method of defence was by "in depth Scattered" in depth.	
			Remainder of month spent in Elementary Training in M.G. work and Recreational Training	
	1st Nov 1917. Dec.			W R Thomson Capt. O.C. 245 M.G. Coy.

Appendices to War Diary of 245 M.G. Coy.
for NOVEMBER 1917.

App: No	Subject, Author &c.
1	50th Div: Order No 140. 31.10.17. The Operation to which previous Warning Order No 139 referred to is postponed. G.S. 50th Div:
2	O.O. No 19. 1.11.17. attached.
3	50th Div: Order No 141. 1.11.17. Reliefs to take place Nov 3, 4 & 5th: 18th Div: to relieve 35th Div: (on left). Nov 6, 7, & 8th: 17th Div: to relieve 57th Div: (on right) Nov 7th: 18th Div: to take over approximately Left Half of 50th Div:? front. Nov 10th: 17th Div: to take over approximately Right Half of 50th Div:? front. G.S. 50th Div:
4	50th Div: Order No 142. 4.11.17. 149 I Bde. to relieve 151 I Bde. in line on night 7/8th inst. G.S. 50th Div:
5	150th I. Bde. O.O. No 135. 9.11.17. 1. 150 I Bde. + 245 MG Coy will move by rail & road to the EPERLECQUES Area on 10th & 11th Nov. 2. Transport to move by road in 2 marches. 3. Personnel to move by train on 11th inst.
6	O.O. No 20. 9.11.17. attached
7	Addendum No 1 to O.O. No 20. 10.11.17. do.

W.P. Thomson Capt:
O.C. 245 M.G. Coy.

<u>SECRET</u>

Operation Order No. 19 by Capt. W.R. Thomson
Comm'd'g 245 M.G. Coy.

BELGIUM 28 N.W. 1/20,000   FRIEDLAND FARM
& Sheet 27 1/40,000.   1st Nov. 1917.

1. The Coy. will move from FRIEDLAND FARM to SUTTON CAMP - F.10.D.6.5 Sheet 27 on 2nd inst. by march route.

2. Move off 2 p.m. Transport will accompany Column.
   Route - DAWSONS CORNER, ELVERDINGHE, DE WIPPE CABARET, INTERNATIONAL CORNER, POPERINGHE - CROMBEKE ROAD.

3. A motor lorry will arrive during the morning to carry packs, valises & Q.M. Stores to SUTTON CAMP. These stores will be on the road outside Camp at 10 A.M.

4 p.m.   W.R. Thomson Capt.
1.11.17.   O.C. 245 M.G. Coy.

(War Diary).

App. 2.

SECRET 7

Operation Order No. 20 by Capt W.R.Thomson
Commd'g 245 M.G. Coy.

Refc: HAZEBROUCK 5A 1/100,000.
BELGIUM 28 NW 1/20,000.
FRANCE 27A, NE, & SE, 1/20,000.

SUTTON CAMP
9th Nov. 17.

---

1.   245 M.G. Coy will move by road and rail on 10th & 11th inst. from SUTTON CAMP to HELLEBROUCK (K.35.a. 27A).

2.   The Transport will move entirely by road in 2 Stages
   (a) SUTTON CAMP to BUYSSCHEURE (Ref: 5A) on 10th inst. Parade to move off at 7·30 A.M. Pass Starting Point (Road Junction 300' S of "P" in PROVEN - Ref: HAZEBROUCK 5A) at 8·20 A.M. Brigade column will be under the Bde. T.O. Capt HUTCHINSON.
       2/LT SEARANCKE will detail a mounted orderly to report to Capt HUTCHINSON at the Starting Point at 8 A.M.
   (b) BUYSSCHEURE to HELLEBROUCQ (27A N.E.) on 11th inst. Under orders to be issued at BUYSSCHEURE.

3.   Baggage wagon will accompany the transport column. Rations for 10th & 11th have been drawn. Those for 12th will be drawn at the end of the journey on afternoon of 11th inst.

4.   The Company will move by train on 11th inst. under orders to be issued later.

5.   A lorry will arrive early in the morning of 11th inst. to carry excess stores to the train. These stores will consist of Officers' valises, Mess utensils, dixies, cooks' materials, orderly room stores. The lorry will be loaded as quickly as possible. Half of the lorry capacity is available.

6.   SUTTON CAMP will be left in a clean and sanitary Condition.

7.   LT. REES with 2 mounted signallers will proceed on 10th inst. by train to HELLEBROUCQ as Advance Party. They will report to Major BAGGE at RTO's Office ELVERDINGHE Stn at 10·30 A.M.

9th Nov/17.
9 P.M.

W.R.Thomson Capt.
O.C. 245 MG Coy.

(War Diary)

Appx 6.

SECRET.   8.

Addendum No 1 to O.O. No 20. by
    Capt W.R. Thomson Commdg 245 M.G. Coy.

Refs: HAZEBROUCK 5A 1/100,000.   SUTTON CAMP
      BELGIUM 28 NW 1/20,000   10º Nov. 17.
      FRANCE 27A, NE & SE.

1.   Refce Para 4 of O.O. No 20. The
Coy. will parade at 10-20 A.M. tomorrow 11th inst.
 MOVE OFF.   10-30 A.M.
 ARRIVE - INTERNATIONAL CORNER   11-30 A.M.
 TRAIN LEAVES   12-25 P.M.

2.   On arrival at WATTEN (HAZEBROUCK
5A & 27A NE) the Coy. will march to HELLEBROUCQ
(about 2½ miles) to billets.

3.   Haversack dinner rations will
be issued before leaving SUTTON CAMP.

4.   4 Cpl BARNES, No 2 Sectn is
detailed to act as guide for the motor lorry.
He will report at 150º Bde. H.Q. SERINGAPATAM CAMP
at 7 A.M. He will accompany the lorry to
2/2nd Northumbrian Field Ambulance where the
front half will be loaded and then he will guide
it to SUTTON CAMP, where a loading party
will be waiting to load the Coy's Stores. This
hour should be about 7-45 A.M.

         Breakfasts will be at 7 AM so
that the dixies and cook's materials will be
ready for loading at 7-45 AM.

10º Nov. 17.   W.R. Thomson Capt.
12-30 P.M.   O.C. 245 M.G. Coy.

(War Diary).

                                          Appx 7.

ORIGINAL

CONFIDENTIAL

WAR DIARY

OF

Nº 245 MACHINE GUN COMPANY

FROM 1ST DECEMBER 1917 TO 31ST DECEMBER 1917

(VOLUME V)

L.W. Rees Lt
for O.C. 245 MGC

WAR DIARY
or
INTELLIGENCE SUMMARY.

(Erase heading not required.)

Army Form C. 2118.

Place	Date	Hour	Summary of Events and Information	Remarks and references to Appendices
HELLEBROUCQ (FRANCE 27A HAZEBROUCK 5A)	Dec. 1st		50th Division on 1 months rest at HELLEBROUCQ in billets. Most time being devoted to Divisional Sports in which all new Comrades. Physique of men much improved. Weather - excellent.	
	6th		Received 50th Divn Warning Order No. 147 - 50th Divn to relieve 33rd Divn in PASSCHENDAELE Sector by 13th Div. leaving the EPERLECQUES Area in 3 Brigade Groups on 10th, 11th, 12th inst. Part of Transport will probably move by road. Divn HQ will move on 13th inst. ? G.O.C will assume Command of the front at noon on that date.	App. 1.
	7th		Received 50th Divn Order No. 148	App. 1
	8th		Received 50th Divn G.X 4924/1 "Organization of Machine Gun Coys in 50th Divn" Received H.Q. Trp. Bde. O.O. No. 223, (249th T.B. Coy.) grouped with this Brigade Group for pur/poses of move.). All information as repeated in R.O. No. 8 made for the move. Attended Conference of all O.C HQ Coy's of Divn with D.H.Q.O of EPERLECQUES discussing formation of Divn M.G. Battalion to make relieving in his easier. All internal work as before- the Coy's being independent Commands. All O.C Coy's of opinion that M.G Battalion would be better. Issued Coy. O.O. No. 24 for move of Coy from EPERLECQUES Area.	App. 2. App. 1. APP 1
	10th		2Lt. SEABROOKE with all Transport with exception of Cooks Cart, Water Cart, H.Q. Limber & Rations Horses proceeded via road from HELLEBROUCQ at 7AM joining 149th Bde. Transport Column at MOULLE to ZERMEZEELE.	

WAR DIARY or INTELLIGENCE SUMMARY

Army Form C. 2118.

Place	Date	Hour	Summary of Events and Information	Remarks and references to Appendices
HELLEBROUCQ	10"		2 Officers from each MG Coy arrived to take over billets. Handed over all Gas Shells etc to them. Lt. REES proceeded on 8 days leave to BAR-LE-DUC. 2 Lewis Guns with bicycles left by train from WATTEN as Advance Party. With 149" Bde Advance Party.	
	11"		Remainder of Transport under Pte GARDNER proceeded from HELLEBROUCQ at 5-30 A.M. joining remainder of Bde Transport Column at MOULLE. By hand route to ST OMER & train to HOPOUTRE (POPERINGHE). Coy paraded at 7-20 A.M. and left HELLEBROUCQ 7-35 A.M. arriving WATTEN Station 8-20 A.M. Entrained immediately and left 9-50 A.M. Arrived BRANDHOEK Stn. 2-15 P.M. Signallers walking & guided Coy to Camp (RIDGE CAMP - G.11.a.2.4. Sheet 28 N.W.) Transport by road under 2nd Lt. SEARANCKE arrived 4.P.M. Transport by rail under Pte GARDNER arrived 7 P.M. Reported arrival to H.Q. 149 Inf Bde in accordance with Operation Orders. Received 149" Inf Bde O.O. N° 224 for move of Coy on 12" instant. repeated in Army O.O. N° 25.	App. 3
RIDGE CAMP Ref. 28.N.W. G.11.a.2.4.	12"		Coy moved from RIDGE CAMP at 1.30 P.M. joining Bde Column at Starting Point, BRANDHOEK, on POPERINGHE- YPRES road. Slow march on account of traffic via VLAMERTINGHE & YPRES to N° 3 Camp POTIJZE (Ref.n BELGIUM Sheet 28 N.W. I.2.d.2.5.). On arrival in dark found that 160 M.G. Coy had not moved out. So had to crowd the men up into s/row tents and shelters in N°s 1, 2 & 3 Camps. Joining linkmen in Camp - remainder with all animals and M.T. SEARANCHE in Lines at G.16.a.1.4. (Transport lines for M.G. Coys not in Line - "B" Echelon)	

WAR DIARY
or
INTELLIGENCE SUMMARY
(Erase heading not required.)

Army Form C. 2118.

Place	Date	Hour	Summary of Events and Information	Remarks and references to Appendices
No.3 MG Camp POTIJZE I.3.a.2.5. (28 N.W.)	13°		Took over Camp from 100th M.G. Coy who marched out at 9 A.M. Fixed men up in the Camp - plenty of accommodation.	
	14°		Went up the Line to M.G. H.Q. (1A & 1B Groups) at TYNE COTTS (see Appendix 4. Map of forward Area) in anticipation of relief of forward guns. Arranged details of relief with O.C. 150 M.G. Coy. at present in line with forward guns. Returned M.G. Group D.O. No 1 (O.M.G.O.) for Relief early morning 16th.	App. 4
	15°		Gave orders to officers for Relief. - 9 gun teams required for forward guns & 2 teams for Anti-Aircraft guns at POMMERN CASTLE. Found Coy. O.O. No. 26 for the Relief. M.G. SEARCHLIGHTS lights 24 inches moved from Lines at BUSSEBOOM to Camp.	App. 5
IN THE LINE Adv. Cy. H.Q. TYNE COTTS	16°		Relieved 150 MG Coy in front line positions by 7 A.M. and in POMMERN CASTLE by 8 A.M. Took over from O.C. 150 MG Coy at HQ MG Coy TYNE COTTS. Positions on right consist of fortified shellholes, a small piece of trench E. of PASSCHENDAELE Road. On left F8-3-6 have good Pill-box - C2 & C3 have good cover in GRAF Ft. Shelter the ruined building.	App. 6
	17°		Position heavily shelled during morning. Pill-box at F8 & F6 smashed in & man killed & 1 badly wounded. Remaining 3 men sent down to Camp "station" in the night. 1 man wounded in F2 position. Can. Brigadier General (144th Bde. in Line) at LEVI COTTS. Obtained his sanction to put 2 guns and have men C2 & C3 pour in a trench occupied by the 14° Div. on right instead of putting 2 new guns & teams in the B16mm in Pill-box. Reported stating to D.H.Q.O. movement of other troops round the positions in daylight.	

WAR DIARY or INTELLIGENCE SUMMARY

Army Form C. 2118.

Place	Date	Hour	Summary of Events and Information	Remarks and references to Appendices
IN THE LINE PASSCHENDAELE Sector	18/9	8 AM	Teams in C.1. & C.3 relieved by teams from Camp. 2 new guns & teams took up position in trench S. of HEETCHEELE - See map.	
			2/Lt PARSONS (16 forward guns on right) did not consider it advisable to throw his teams owing to the difficulty of getting reliefs out & the probability of teams going astray on the ground today. No positions had been in touch down blown away by the shelling of the 17th inst. LT REES returned from leave 5 days at Bar-le-duc	
	19th		OR. 157 M.G. Coy arrived to take over arrangements for reliefs. Received M.G. Group O.O. N°2. (Issued by 9.S.S.O. Dut.) for the relief tonight. See Appy. O.O. N° 27 for relief of forward guns by 151. MG Coy in early morning 20th inst.	App? 7
	20th		All teams relieved by 8 A.M. and returned to N° 3 Camp. POTIJZE. in night. 149 MG Coy reported relief of barrage guns complete at 9 A.M. Reported relief complete to O.H.G.O. in person at 10 A.M.	
	21st		2 men to 2/A West French Zouf - they were in forward posn on nights for 4 days. Forwarded report to O.H.G.O. (? no wonder so hot feed.) 2 men sick with Gas.	
	22nd		Received 50th Divn D.O. N° 153 for M.G. Group's relief. Found Coy D.O. N° 28 for relief of barrage guns "B" Group by 24.5 MG Coy on early morning of 24th inst. 2/Lt DERBYSHIRE guns in relieve to W.K. & OR transport from M.G. Coy O.H.G.O. enquired Provisional H.Q. Byrnes listening for 50th Divl Sectr.	Appx 8/9
	23rd		(PASSCHENDAELE Sector). Ft. Hannis MG to all "German" guns team Officers. Apparently it is reported that the enemy will attempt an attack in this Sector. All prisoners taken up to date state that the enemy has no intention	App? 10

Army Form C. 2118.

WAR DIARY
or
INTELLIGENCE SUMMARY.
(Erase heading not required.)

Instructions regarding War Diaries and Intelligence Summaries are contained in F. S. Regs., Part II. and the Staff Manual respectively. Title pages will be prepared in manuscript.

Place	Date	Hour	Summary of Events and Information	Remarks and references to Appendices
IN THE LINE PASSCHENDAELE Sector (Rest 28 mts)	24	8 pm	Relief of barrage positions completed. Lt. REES & 1/2 "B" group at TYNE COTTS. Weather very frosty, ground hard.	
	25		Received D.M.G.O. to return to Company to base & 27 ORs	APP 10
	26	5 am	Capt. W. R. Thurnam proceeds to Base Rest Station 6th Corps Rest Station POPERINGHE (sick) Received 27 ORs proceeds to Base O.O. No 135 for M.G. group relief. Received 56 Div O.O. 28 Gunners Coy O.O. 28	App 11
		8.45 a.m.	B group positions received attention with shell gas	
	28	8 pm	Relief of barrage positions completed & teams returned to Camp at POTIJZE 2/Lt PARSONS proceeds on leave to U.K. Received D.M.C.O. 6 x 2 in connection with M.G. Helium scheme	App 11
	29	3 am	6 ORs to hospital (gas)	
			2/Lt GRAVES and TEAGUE returned with 35 ORs & the complete equipment & mules of M.G. section from the U.K.	
	30	Noon	Received 50 Div. O.O. 156 for M.G. relief 2 ORs to hospital (gas)	App 12

WAR DIARY
or
INTELLIGENCE SUMMARY.

Army Form C. 2118.

Place	Date	Hour	Summary of Events and Information	Remarks and references to Appendices
IN THE LINE PASSCHENDAELE SECTOR (SHEET 28 NE)	31	5pm	Issued Op. O. 30 for relief of A portion front by 2nd M.G. Coy.	APP 13.

R. W. Ross Lt
2i/c O.C. 2nd M.G. Coy

31st Decr 1917.

APPX N° 1

50TH DIVISION ORDER. N° 148.

4TH DEC. 1917.

1. The 50th Division (less Divisional Artillery) will relieve the 33rd Division in the line by the 13th December, 1917.

2. The 50th Division will move from EPERLECQUES Area in accordance with attached movement table.
Supply Sections of Companies of the Train will move under the orders of O.C. Divisional Train.

3. The following distances will be maintained on the march.
   Between Companies . . . . 100 yards
   Between Unit & its Transport . . . . 100 yards
   Between Battalions . . . . 500 yards
   When Transport is Brigaded.
      Between Each Battalion Transport . . . . 100 yards
   A distance of 100 yards will be maintained between every six vehicles.

4. (a) The 150th Infantry Brigade will relieve the 98th Infantry Brigade in the line on the night of 12/13th December, under arrangements to be made direct between the Brigade Commanders concerned.

   (b) The 150th & 151st M.G. Coys, will relieve the 100th & 248th M.G. Coys on the night of the 11th/12th December, under arrangements to be made direct between the D.M.G.O's concerned.

5. All troops of the 50th Division, on arrival in 33rd Divisional Area, will come under the orders of the G.O.C. 33rd Division.

6. The Command will pass from G.O.C. 33rd Division to G.O.C. 50th Division at 12 noon 13th December, 1917, when 50th Divisional Headquarters will close at EPERLECQUES and open at the RAMPARTS, MENIN GATE, YPRES.

Copy to 245 Machine Gun Coy.

SECRET.

Operation Order No 24 by Capt. W. R. Thomson
Comm'dg 245 M. G. Coy.

Ref: France 27A 1/20,000
 " HAZEBROUCK 5A 1/100,000
 " BELGIUM 28 N.W. 1/20,000.

HELLEBROUCQ
9. 12. 17.

---

1.   The 245" M. G. Coy. will proceed from HELLEBROUCQ in the 149" Inf. Bde. Group to BRANDHOEK G. 11. a. 2. 4 Sheet 28 N. W. on 11" Dec. 17.
     Transport will move under orders issued in Addendum No 1.

2.   The Coy. will parade on 11.12.17. to move off at 7.35 A.M.
     Entrain WATTEN 8.20 A.M. Train leaves about 9 A.M. and will arrive BRANDHOEK about 2 p.m.

3.   Billets at HELLEBROUCQ will be left clean and handed over to the Area Commandant or a relieving M. G. Coy.

4.   CORP'L MITCHELL with 1 Signaller (with bicycles) will proceed by train from WATTEN at 8.30 A.M. on 10" inst. to BRANDHOEK as Advance Party.

5.   SERG'T. JOYCE with 4 men will remain behind at HELLEBROUCQ as Rear Party. They will entrain at WATTEN at 8.30 A.M. on 12" inst. and rejoin the Coy. at POTIJZE (Ref: 28 N.W.). on evening of 12" inst.

6.   A motor lorry (to be shared with 446" Coy R.E) will arrive at Coy. H.Q. during evening of 11" inst. This will convey blankets & stores to WATTEN. The C. S. M. will detail 1 Corp'l & 3 men to proceed with this lorry to guard the stores after unloading at the Station.

7.   A motor lorry will meet the Coy. on arrival at BRANDHOEK to convey these stores to Camp.

Issued at 7 p.m.
9° Dec. 17.

W R Thomson Capt.
O. C. 245 M. G. Coy.

Copies to   1. Office (promulgated to Coy.)
            2.
            3. } War Diary.

App.x No 4

APPX N°4

SECRET.

Copy No. 4.

Appendix No. 1 to Coy. O.O. No. 24

MOVE OF TRANSPORT.

1. The Transport under 2/Lt. SEARANCKE will move on 10th inst. by road with the exception of H.Q. Limber, Cook's Cart, Water cart and officers chargers which will proceed as detailed in Para. 5.

2. The Column will pass the Starting Point (MOULLE Q.11.c.5.8. Sheet 27A S.E.) at 9-40 A.M. where it will join the Brigade Transport Column under O.C. No. 2 Coy Div'l Train A.S.C.

3. The column will proceed via SERQUES and halt for the night at ZERMEZEELE (Ref. HAZEBROUCQ 5A).

   On the 11th the column will proceed via POPERINGHE to BRANDHOEK where a guide from the Coy. will be waiting.

4. 2 Riding Horses will accompany the column.

5. The remaining transport detailed in Para 1. will move on 11th inst. passing Starting Point (MOULLE - Q.11.C.2.1. - Sheet 27A S.E.) at 6.20 A.M.

   Driver GARDNER will be in charge, & will report to O.C. Column at S.P.

   This Column will entrain at ST. OMER & detrain at HOPOUTRE. (POPERINGHE) joining the Coy. at BRANDHOEK.

6. All detachments of the Coy. will report their arrival in Camp to O.C.

Issued at 4 p.m.   W. R. Thomson Capt.
9. 12. 17.   O.C. 245 M.G. Coy.

Copies to   1.   2/Lt. SEARANCKE
             2.   Dr. GARDNER (extracts).
             3.   Office.
             4. } War Diary.
             5. }

APPX. Nº 2
50TH DIVISION
G.X.4924/1.

ORGANIZATION OF MACHINE GUN COMPANIES IN 50TH DIVISION.

1. Machine Gun Companies will be grouped & distributed in 3 Echelons.
   (a). In the line — "A" and "B" Group.
   (b). "A" ECHELON — POTIJZE.
   (c). "C" ECHELON — BRANDHOEK.

2. "A" Group. 12 guns in front line system.
   "B" Group. 12 guns for Barrage.

3. O.C. Machine Gun Company "A" Group will command all guns in the line and is responsible to the Brigadier-General Commanding in the line.
   "B" Group is commanded by the 2nd in Command of the Company.

4. RELIEF.
   (a). Gun Personnel. Companies work in pairs — Pairs relieve each other every 4 days; within each pair, the Companies alternately man "A" and "B" Group.
   (b). Transport
   Transport of the pair of Companies in the line takes duty during the 4 days tour of their own Companies in the line, Each transport undertaking all duties on alternate days.
   The Transport of the Companies out of the line moves back to BRANDHOEK, being in rest for 4 days.
   Transport duty is from 10 A.M. - 10 A.M.

5. Signallers will be pooled.
   Communications as follow:-
   (A.1.) Sections, by runner to Group H.Q.
   (A.2.) Batteries, by Telephone to Group H.Q.
   (b). Group H.Qr. to Brigade H.Q. & Divl H.Qrs.
   (c). M.G. Report Centre established at "A" Echelon.
   (d). All messages for Companies are sent to Report Centre for distribution.
   Two runners to be retained permanently.
   Messages for line are sent up normally with rations, or through D.R.L.S, or special runner, if urgent.

6. "A" ECHELON

   (a). 4 Camps each sufficient for 1 Company.
   (b). 2 bricked Transport Standings.
   (c). Personnel of 2 Companies in rest, & details of 2 Companies in line permanently camped here.
   (d). Quartermaster Stores.

7. "B" ECHELON

   (a). Camp for Transport & Transport personnel of 2 resting Companies.
   (b). All riding animals.
   (c). Rest Camp for 1 officer and 10 men per Company.
   (d). 2 cooks & 1 cycle orderly.

8. The following temporary appointments have been made. Duties will be assumed at the places stated on arrival in the new Area.

   1. Quartermaster.   Lt. Morrison, 150th M.G. Coy POTIJZE.
   2. A/Qr. Master   Lt. Fletcher, 149th M.G. Coy   "
   3. Clerk.   Pte Jackson, 245 M.G. Coy   "
   4. Adjutant.   Capt. Staughton 245 M.G. Coy DIV. H.Q. MENIN GATE.
   5. Orderly Room Sergeant. Sgt. Cairns, 149th M.G. Coy   " "

9. All Returns will be submitted to the D.M.G.O.'s Office from the 13th instant, inclusive.

                        (Signed). J.S. Harper.
                                   Major
                              D.M.G.O.

8th December 1917.

SECRET.   APPX No 3

Copy No 3

Operation Order No 25 by Capt W.R.Thomson
Commdg 245 M.G. Coy.

Refce BELGIUM 28 N.W. 1/20,000.   RIDGE CAMP
BRANDHOEK.
11° Dec. 17.

1. 245 M.G. Coy. will move in the 149°. Inf. Bde. Group from BRANDHOEK to No 3 Camp POTIJZE I.3.d.2.5. tomorrow 12° inst.

2. Parade to move off at 1-30 p.m.
Route :- RIDGE CAMP, Main POPERINGHE-YPRES Road, VLAMERTINGHE, YPRES, MENIN GATE, ZONNEBEKE-ROAD.

3. Fighting Limbers & 2 Riding Horses will accompany the column.

The remaining Transport will move to Bricked Standings at G.16.a.1.4. tomorrow immediately after the departure of the Coy.

These lines will be permanently allotted to the Coy. Fighting Limbers will remain at POTIJZE and when the Coy. is in the line (every 4 days alternate commencing from night 15/16° inst.) 24 mules will stay in lines at POTIJZE.

The Transport officer will accompany the fighting limber mules staying alternately at No 3 Camp and the permanent lines.

11 p.m.   W R Thomson Capt
11.12.17.   O.C. 245 M.G. Coy.

Copies to   1. Office
2. 2/Lt. SEARANCKE
3.
4. } War Diary

Appx. No 5

MACHINE GUN GROUP 50TH DIVISION
OPERATION ORDER No 1.

DEC. 14TH 17.

1. The 245 Machine Gun Company will relieve the 150th Machine Gun Company in "A" Group. and anti-aircraft positions at POMMERN CASTLE.
   The 149th Machine Gun Company will relieve the 151st Machine Gun Company, in "B" Group. on the night 15/16th December 1917.

2. Guns only will be taken in by the relieving Companies. All tripods, Ammunition, & Trench Stores to be handed over.

3. All details of relief to be arranged between Company Commanders concerned.

4. Relief of "A" Group to be completed by dawn of 16th inst.

5. Relief of "B" Group to be completed by 8 A.M. on the 16th inst.

6. On Completion of relief Capt. W.R. Thomson O/C. 245 Machine Gun Company will assume command of all guns in "A & B" Groups.

7. Handing over certificates to be rendered to Quartermasters Office by 2 p.m. on 16th inst.

8. Completion of relief to be reported by the Code word. "EMMA".

Copy to 245 Machine Gun Coy.

APPX n° 6

Copy

N° 245 M.G. Coy.   O.O n° 26
by Capt. W. R. Thomson
15-12-17

1. N° 245 M.G Coy will relieve the N° 150 M.G. Coy in A Group and AA positions at POMMERN CASTLE on the night of 15/16 Dec 1917.

2. Guns only will be taken in all tripods, SAA and trench stores will be handed over by the 150th M.G. Coy

3. Relief to be completed by 6 AM.

4. 2/LT ATTWATER with 5 guns will relieve the LEFT SECTOR
2/LT PARSONS with 6 guns will relieve the RIGHT Sector
2/LT LEE with 2 guns will relieve at POMMERN CASTLE

(sgd) W. R Thomson Capt

APPX 7

MACHINE GUN GROUP. 50TH DIVISION
OPERATION ORDER No 2
18TH DEC. 1917.

1. The 151st Machine Gun Company will relieve the 245th Machine Gun Company in "A" Group, and anti-aircraft positions at POMMERN CASTLE, and the 150th Machine Gun Company will relieve the 149th Machine Gun Company in "B" Group on the night of 19/20th December 1917.

2. Guns only will be taken in by the relieving Companies.
All Tripods, Ammunition, Trench Stores, maps & photographs to be handed over.

3. All details of relief to be arranged between Company Commanders concerned.

4. Relief of "A" Group to be completed by dawn 20th inst.

5. Relief of "B" Group to be completed by 8. am of 20th inst.

6. On Completion of relief Capt. D. Halston, 151st Machine Gun Company will assume command of all guns in "A" & "B" Groups.

7. Handing over certificates to be rendered to Quartermaster Office by 2.0. p.m. on 25th inst.

8. Completion of relief to be wired in "B. A B" Code to Brigade Headquarters in the line and to D.M.G.O.

9. On relief, 245th & 149th Machine Gun Companies will return to Nos. 3 & 4 Camps POTIJZE. Respectively.

10. Transport personnel of 150th & 151st Machine Gun Companies will relieve that of 149th & 245th Machine Gun Companies at POTIJZE by 12 noon, 20th inst.
On relief, the transport personnel of the latter Companies will proceed to BRANDHOEK.

Copy to 245 Machine Gun Coy.

APPX NO 8

SECRET

50TH DIVISION OPERATION ORDER No 153

22ND DEC. 1917.

1. The 149th Machine Gun Company will relieve the 151st Machine Gun Company in "A" Group, & the 245th Machine Gun Company will relieve the 150th Machine Gun Company in "B" Group on the night of 23rd/24th December 1917.

2. Guns only will be taken in by the relieving Companies. All Tripods, Ammunition, Trench stores, Maps and Photographs to be handed over.

3. All details of relief to be arranged between Company Commanders concerned.

4. Relief of "A" Group to be completed by dawn 24th inst.

5. Relief of "B" Group to be completed by 8 A.M on 24th instant.

6. On completion of relief, Major T. Morris D.S.O., 149th Machine Gun Company, will assume command of all guns in "A" & "B" Groups.

7. Handing over certificates to be rendered to Quartermasters office by 2.0 p.m. 24th inst.

8. Completion of relief to be wired in "B.A.B" Code to Brigade Headquarters in the line & to D.M.G.O.

9. On relief 150th & 151st Machine Gun Companies will return to Nos 1 and 2 Camps POTIJZE respectively.

10. Transport personnel of 149th and 245th Machine Gun Companies will relieve that of the 150th and 151st Machine Gun Companies at POTIJZE by 12 noon, 24th instant.
On relief Transport personnel of the latter Companies will proceed to BRANDHOEK.

Copy to 245 Machine Gun Company.

COPY

Copy

No 245. M.G. Coy   O.O. 27
by Capt W.R Thomson
                    19.12.17

1. No 151 M.G Coy will relieve the
   No 245 M.G Coy in B. Group on
   night of 27/28 Dec 1917
2. Guns & spare parts only will
   be brought out by the relieved
   Coy
3. Guides will report at TYNE
   COTT at 6 AM. 28/12/17
4. OH relief teams will
   return to No 3 Camp POTIJZE

                (Sgd) W.R.Thomson
                            Capt

Copy   App: No 9

No 245 M.G. Coy   O.O No 28
by Capt W.R. Thomson
                     22/12/17

1. No 245 M.G. Coy will relieve No 150 M.G. Coy in B. Group on the morning of 24.12.1917
2. Guns & spare parts only will be taken in by the relieving teams. Tripods, S.A.A. & belt boxes & trench stores will be taken over from the relieved teams.
3. Relief to be complete by 6.30 A.M.
4. Relief complete to be reported proforma to Group HQ by Section officers of relieving teams
5. 2/Lt Lee will take command of B Group.

2/Lt Parsons & 4 guns will take over S position
2/Lt Attwater & 4 guns together with 2 guns & teams attached from N° 149 M.G. Coy will take over D Battery
2/Lt Lee & 4 guns will take over C Battery.

6. Guides will be provided by the relieved teams & will be at TYNE COTT at 6.15 A.M.

7. Rations for two days will be taken in together with water.

8. 2/Lt Seasonche will arrange for pack animals to transport guns, rations, etc to TYNE COTT.

          (sgd) W. B. Thomann
                    Capt

SECRET.

APPENDIX No 1. TO 50TH DIVISION PROVINCIAL DEFENCE INSTRUCTIONS.

MACHINE GUN DEFENCE.

1. The locations of Machine Guns.
   (a). In the line.
   (b). On the Crest Farm line
   (c). On barrage lines.
   (d). On the Divisional Reserve line.

   are shewn in map "C".

2. In the event of a hostile attack developing on the 50th, or either of the neighbouring Divisional fronts, the O.C. Machine Guns in the will get into immediate touch with the Brigade Commander, & Section officers into touch with the nearest Battalion or Company Commanders.

3. If our front system in the neighbourhood of Passchendaele is captured by the enemy & Crest Farm line becomes the front line:—
   (a). "C" Battery will shorten barrage to line Passchendaele Church - D 6 Central.
   (b). "B" Battery will continue on its present barrage lines.

4. In the event of the withdrawal of our line to HAALEN SUPPORT:—
   (a) "C" Battery will
      (i). Reinforce the HAALEN SUPPORT LINE with 1 gun firing N & 1 gun firing N.E.
      (ii). Cover the line against attack from E & SE by means of 2 guns withdrawn to vicinity of concrete Mebus. D. 11. d. 30.45.
   (b). "B" Battery will switch barrage lines to GRAF WOOD - CROSS ROADS - CREST FARM.
   (c). The 2 reserve guns at TYNE COTS, will cover the area DASH CROSSING - KEERSELAARHOEK

5. In event of the Divisional Reserve (ABRAHAM HEIGHTS) line becoming our main line of defence:—

5. (a). "B" Battery will hand over the concrete Mebus at D.17.a.2.9. to an infantry Garrison & will place:-
    (i) 2 guns in vicinity of HAMBURG.
    (ii). 2 guns at TYNE COTS.

In event of a S.O.S. signal being given on the 50th Divisional or either of the neighbouring Divisional fronts, the duty Company POTIJZE will stand to & be ready to:-

(a). Reinforce the Divisional Reserve (ABRAHAM HEIGHTS) LINE with four guns on the line BEECHAM - ABRAHAM HEIGHTS.

(b) Occupy a Barrage position at D.16.C.6.4. (4 guns). with lines as follows.
    (i). If covering BELLEVUE SWITCH line, Barrage lines on D.12.C.25.65 DECK WOOD.
    (ii). If covering Divisional Reserve line (ABRAHAM HEIGHTS), Barrage lines on SNIPE HALL - BELLEVUE (inclusive).

(c). Occupy a barrage position at SPRINGFIELD D.16.C.10.05. (4 guns) with lines as follows;-
    (i). If covering BELLEVUE SWITCH line, Barrage lines on DECK WOOD - FRIESLAND.
    (ii). If covering Divisional Reserve line (ABRAHAM HEIGHTS), Barrage lines on BELLEVUE. D4.d.20.35.

In the event of our line being forced in direction of DASH CROSSING - DARING CROSSING, both (b). & (c). will protect the Southern flank of the Division with direct fire.

(d). Company Headquarters will be established at SPRINGFIELD.

(e). The remaining Company at POTIJZE will stand to & await further orders.

7. The moves detailed in para 6 will not take place until orders to that effect are received from the D.M.G.O.

8. The following amount of ammunition will be maintained
(a). Front System guns — 12 belt boxes per gun
(b). Battery positions — 16 " " and 30,000 rounds S.A.A. per battery.
(c). S. Guns (located on Divisional Reserve line) — 10 Belt boxes & 3000 S.A.A. per gun

APP.x N.o 10

MACHINE GUN DEFENCE SCHEME.

1. Possible enemy action
   (a). Local surprise attacks to recapture Passchendaele
   (b). Stronger attack to pinch off Passchendaele Salient.
   (c). Large operation against Second Army front.
   Note Southern Group is the danger.

2. In event of withdrawal of our line to CREST FARM SWITCH.
   (a). C. Battery will shorten barrage to line PASSCHENDAELE. C.H.D.6. Central.
   (b). B. Battery will continue

3. In event of withdrawal of our line to HAALEN SWITCH.
   (a). C Battery will (1). Reinforce switch line with 2 guns, firing N.E. & N.
   (2) Cover switch line against attack from E and S.E. with 2 guns in vicinity of pill box.
   (b). B. Battery will switch to barrage line GRAF WOOD Cross roads. CREST FARM.
   (c). Two reserve guns TYNE COTS will cover area DASH CROSSING KEERSELAARHOEK.

4. In event of withdrawal to ABRAHAM HEIGHT SWITCH.
   (a). B. Battery will hand over the pill box to our Infantry garrison & fall back:-
   (1). 2 guns to vicinity of HAMBURG.
   (2). 2 guns to TYNE COTS.

5. In the event of attack on Passchendaele the duty Coy at POTIJZE will stand to and be ready to.
   (a). Reinforce the ABRAHAM HEIGHTS switch with four guns.
   (b). Occupy a barrage position at D.16.c.6.4. with line on D.12.c.25.65. DECK WOOD with four guns.

5. (c). Occupy a barrage position at SPRINGFIELD. D.16.C.10.05. with line on DECK WOOD. FRIESLAND.
In the event of our line being forced in direction of DASH CROSSING DARING Crossing, both (b) & (c). will protect the S. flank of the DIV. with direct fire.
(d). Coy. HQs will be established at SPRINGFIELD.
(e). The remaining Coy at POTIJZE will stand to and await further orders.

6. In event of attack the O.C. Machine Guns in line will get into immediate touch with Brigade Commander & each Section Officer with nearest Coy in Bn Command.

7. All gun Nos must now
(a). No & field of fire of gun.
(b). Position & fields of fire of flanking guns.
(c). Position of Infantry Posts to front & flanks.
(d). Position of M.G. Section H.Q. & Group. H.Q.
(e). Position of Bn. & Bgde HQs.
(f). Names of localities in immediate front.

8. Ammunition to be Maintained.
(a). Front line guns 12 boxes per gun.
(b). Battery position 16 belt boxes per gun & 30.000. S.A.A. per Battery.
(c). S. Guns 10 belts & 5 boxes S.A.A per gun.

9. Temporary Range cards will be made at each position.

M.G. 97.   APP.No 10A

MOVE OF SURPLUS PERSONNEL OF 245 M.G.Coy
26.12.17.

Parade at 5 A.M.

One limbered G.S. Wagon will be detailed by T.O. 245 Machine Gun Company to carry Mens Kit etc to POPERINGHE STATION.

Rations for 27th will be carried

2Lt N. FLETCHER. 149 Machine Gun Company will march the party and report to R.T.O. POPERINGHE by 8. A.M.

On completion of duty he will hand over charge of party to SGT TINDLE. R.J. of 245 Machine Gun Company, together with nominal Roll, AF's B.122 and movement order.

Party will be in possession of full Kit, blankets etc.

(Signed) J.R. Staughton Capt.
for D.M.G.O.
50th Division

25.12.17.

SECRET

50TH DIVISION OPERATION ORDER No. 155.

26TH DEC. 1917.

1. The 150th Machine Gun Company will relieve the 149th Machine Gun Company in A. Group, & the 151st Machine Gun Company will relieve the 245th Machine Gun Company in B. Group on the night of 27th/28th December 1917.

2. Guns only will be taken in by the relieving Companies. All Tripods, Ammunition, Trench Stores, Maps & Photographs to be handed over.

3. All details of relief to be arranged between Company Commanders concerned.

4. Relief of "A" Group to be completed by dawn on 28th inst.

5. Relief of "B" Group to be completed by 8 A.m. on 28th instant.

6. On completion of relief Captain G.R. McPhail, O.C. 150th Machine Gun Company will assume command of all guns in "A" & "B" Groups.

7. Handing over certificates to be rendered to Quartermasters' Office by 2.0 P.M. 28th inst.

8. Completion of relief to be wired in "B.A.B." Trench Code to Brigade Headquarters in the line and to D.M.G.O.

9. On relief 245th & 149th Machine Gun Companies will return to Nos. 3 and 4 Camp POTIJZE respectively.

10. Transport personnel of 150th & 151st Machine Gun Companies will relieve that of 149th & 245th Machine Gun Companies, at POTIJZE by 12 noon 28th instant. On relief transport personnel of the latter Companies will proceed to BRANDHOEK.

Copy to :- 245. Machine Gun Company.

Appx No 11

No 245 MACHINE GUN COY. OPERATION ORDER No 29.
By CAPTAIN W.R. THOMSON

26.12.17

1. No 245 Machine Gun Company will be relieved by No 151 Machine Gun Company, in "B" Group. On the night of 27/28th Dec 1917.

2. Guns & spare parts only will be taken out by the relieving teams.

3. Relief to be complete by 8 A.M. on 28/12/17.

4. On relief No 245 Machine Gun Company will return to No 3 Camp POTIJZE.

(Signed) W.R. Thomson
Capt.
O.C. 245 M.G. Coy.

G.X/2.   APP^x N°11^A

245 M.G. Company.

Ref: M.G. Defence Scheme.

1. Whilst in reserve 149 & 245 M.G. Companies will be on duty as follows —

   28th inst   245 M.G. Company.
   29th "   149 "   "
   30th "   245 "   "
   31st "   149 "   "

   Period of duty from 6 a.m. — 6 a.m.

2. In the event of the Duty Company having to proceed to re-inforce the ABRAHAM HEIGHTS SWITCH, a carrying party of 1 N.C.O & 30 men will be attached to the Duty Company from the non-duty Company. This party will rejoin their Company in reserve on completion of their task.

3. O.C. Companies will requisition on transport as follows:—

   149 M.G. Coy   from   151 M.G. Coy.
   245 "   "   "   150 "   "

   Draught animals only and <u>not</u> pack transport will be demanded.

28.12.17.

Signed J.S. Harper Lt Col.
D.M.G.O 50th Div.

APPX. No. 12

50TH DIVISION OPERATION ORDER No. 156

30TH DEC. 1917

1. The 245th Machine Gun Company will relieve the 150th Machine Gun Company on "A" Group, & the 149th Machine Gun Company will relieve the 151st Machine Gun Company in "B" Group on the night of 31st December 1917/1st January 1918.

2. Guns only will be taken in by the relieving Companies.
   All Tripods, ammunition, Trench Stores, Maps & photographs to be handed over.

3. All details of relief to be arranged between the Company Commanders concerned.

4. Relief of "A" Group to be completed by dawn of January 1st 1918.

5. Relief of "B" Group to be completed by 8 A.M. January 1st 1918.

6. On completion of relief, Capt. I.R. Houghton, 245th Machine Gun Company, will assume command of all guns in "A" & "B" Groups.

7. Handing over certificates to be rendered to Quartermaster's Office by 2 pm January 1st 1918.

8. Completion of relief to be rendered in "B.A.B." Code to Brigade H.Q. in the line & to D.M.G.O.

9. On relief 150th & 151st Machine Gun Companies will proceed to Nos 1 & 2 Camps respectively, at POTIJZE.

10. Transport personnel of 245th & 149th Machine Gun Companies will relieve that of 150th & 151st Machine Gun Companies at POTIJZE, by 12 noon, Jan 1st 1918. On relief transport personnel of 150th & 151st Machine Gun Companies will proceed to BRANDHOEK.

Copy to 245 Machine Gun Coy.

App.x No. 13

COMPANY OPERATION ORDER No. 39.

DEC 31ST 1917.

1. The 245th Machine Gun Company will relieve the 150th Machine Gun Company in "A" Group on the night of 31st Dec. 17 & 1st Jan 1918.

2. Guns & spare parts only will be taken in by relieving teams. Tripods, S.A.A, & belt boxes, & trench stores will be taken over.

3. Relief to be complete by dawn of 1/1/18

4. Relief complete to be reported personally to Group. H.Q. by Section Officer of 149 Coy.

5. 2/LT. KEAWS 151 Coy with 6 guns & 5 gun teams (1 gun to be kept at Section H.Q. in reserve) will relieve F.1. F.2. F.3. F.4. & C.1. position in the Right sector.
He will parade at 12. AM. 1/1/18. Guides (one per gun) from 150 Machine Gun Company will be detailed to guide the relieving teams to the positions from TYNE COTTS.

6. 2/LT LEE. with 5 guns & 4 gun teams (1 gun in reserve at Section H.Q). will relieve F.5. F.6. C.2. C.3 position in the left Sector. He will parade at 12.15 AM. Guide from 150 Machine Gun Company will conduct this party from TYNE COTTS to gun positions.

7. Rations. Two days rations and 1 Petrol tin of water per team will be taken in.

8. Transport. 2/Lt Searancke will arrange for 6 mules for each party to carry the guns and rations.

9. ROUTE. POTIJZE. MULE TRACK. TYNE COTTS.

10. Acknowledge.

Issued at 11.30 AM.

Copy to 245 M.G. Coy

ORIGINAL

CONFIDENTIAL

WAR DIARY

OF

No 245 MACHINE GUN COMPANY

From 1st JANUARY 1918 TO 31st JANUARY 1918

(VOLUME VI.)

L.R. Thomson Captⁿ
O.C. 245 MG Coy

Army Form C. 2118.

WAR DIARY
or
INTELLIGENCE SUMMARY.

(Erase heading not required.)

Instructions regarding War Diaries and Intelligence Summaries are contained in F. S. Regs., Part II. and the Staff Manual respectively. Title pages will be prepared in manuscript.

Place	Date	Hour	Summary of Events and Information	Remarks and references to Appendices
POTIJZE I.3.A.25.	JAN 2		Received O.O. No.1 from D.M.G.O. relative to move to STEENVOORDE. Group HQrs in the line moved from TYNE COTT to DAN HO.	APPX N° 1
	3	2 AM	Guns being in "A" Group relieved at 2 A.M. 21/LT GROVES took over R/Section from HUTHEENS sent to this Company by 151 Machine Gun Company.	
		10 AM	Lt REES attended conference of D.M.G.O. and Company Commanders relative to move out of line and proposed Programme of work while on Rest.	
	5	9 PM	Company moved by motor to STEENVOORDE.	
STEENVOORDE Q.1.C.12. Sheet 27	10		Received O.O. NO 159 from D.M.G.O relative to move to WESTBECOURT	APPX N° 2
	15	9 PM	Transport proceeded by road, halting for the night 15/16th January in the RENESCURE Staging area.	
	16	10.45	Company moved by train to WESTBECOURT, entraining at GODEWAERSVELDE and detraining at WIZERNES.	APPX N° 3
WESTBECOURT V.M.Q. 20.90 Sheet 27 R5E	24		Received 50th DIV. O.O. N° 161 from D.M.G.O. relative to move to POTIJZE	APPX N° 4
	26		Received 50th DIV. O.O. N° 163 from D.M.G.O. temporary command of the Company during the absence of Captain Thomson.	APPX N° 5
	29	10.35 AM	The Transport proceeded by road, halting for the night 29/30th January in the OUDEZEELE Staging area.	APPX N° 6
	30	6 AM	The Company moved by rail to POTIJZE, entraining at WIZERNES and detraining at Y.PRES.	
POTIJZE I.3.d.25.	31		Received 50th DIV. O.O. N° 166 from D.M.G.O. Guns being in "B" Group relieved by 245 Machine Gun Company on the night of 31st Jan/1st Feby 1918.	APPX N° 7

W.R. Thomson Capt.
O.C. 2nd 50th M.G. Coy.

APPx 1.

MACHINE GUN GROUP 50TH DIVISION.

OPERATION ORDER No 1.

1. The 245th and 149th Machine Gun Companies will be relieved by two Companies of the 33rd Division, on the night of 4/5th Jan. 1918.

2. Relief of "A" Group (245th M.G. Coy) to be complete by 5 A.M.

3. Relief of "B" Group (149th M.G. Coy) to be complete by 7 A.M.

4. Guns and spare parts only will be taken in by the relieving Companies. All Tripods, ammunition, Trench Stores, Maps & Photographs to be handed over.

5. Handing over receipts will be rendered as early as possible on the morning of the 5th inst. to Quartermaster Stores.

6. Completion of relief to be wired in "AA" Code to Brigade HQrs in the line and to D.M.G.O.

7. The Command of all M.G. in the area will pass to D.M.G.O. 33rd Division at 10 a.m. 5th inst.

8. Each Company will hand over 50,000 rounds S.A.A. in clips to the Companies in 33rd Division, taking over in POT IJZE Camp and will take over 50,000 rounds on arrival in new area from 33rd Div.

9. The 150th and 151st Companies will complete the complement of Guns, Tripods, belt boxes, etc from the 245th and 149th Companies respectively by 5 pm 3rd inst.

10. Receipts will be obtained by all Companies of any stores etc handed over to 33rd Division at POTIJZE Camp.
Receipts to be handed into Q.M. Stores by the 6th inst.

11. In the new area M.G. Coys will be accommodated as follows:-

 149th Coy   WATOU
 150th "   WINNEZEELE.
 151st "   EECKE.
 245th "   STEENVOORDE.

12. Movement order attached, times of trains will be notified later.

13. Acknowledge.

Copy to 245th M.G. Coy

(Signed) J.S.Harper,
Lt Col.
D.M.G.O.
50th Division

SECRET. APPX N° 2.

50TH DIVISION OPERATION ORDER
N° 159.
9.1.18.

Reference Map, Sheet 5A
HAZEBROUCK. 1/100,000.

1. The 50th Division will move from the STEENVOORDE area to the TILQUES Area between the 16th & 19th January, in accordance with the attached table.

2. Brigade Groups will be constituted as under.

149th Infantry Brigade Group.	150th Infantry Brigade Group.	151st Infantry Brigade Group.
149th Inf Bde.	150th Inf Bde.	151st Inf Bde.
7th Field Coy R.E.	245th M.G. Coy.	No. 3 Coy. Div. Train.
No. 2 Coy. Div. Train.	No. 4 Coy. Div. Train.	1/1 Nbn. Field Amb.
1/2nd Nbn. Field Amb.	1/3 Nbn. Field Amb.	Div. Salvage Coy.
		244 Employment Coy.
		1/1 Nbn. M.V.S.

4. The Machine Gun Coys will be billeted in WESTBECOURT, less the 150th Machine Gun Coy at SETQUES.

5. Entraining and detraining arrangements will be made by "Q."

6. The 50th Division will be in G.H.Q Reserve on arrival in the TILQUES Area and will be ready to move by road or rail at 48 hours notice.

7. 50th Divisional Headquarters will close at STEENVOORDE at 10.0 a.m. 19th January and reopen at the same hour at WIZERNES.

8. Acknowledge.

(Sgd) J.A. KENTISH Capt
for Lt. Col.
G.S.
General Staff
50th DIVISION

Issued at 8 p.m.

Appx N³ Copy N° 3.

245 MACHINE GUN COMPANY

OPERATION ORDER N° 32.
13. 1. 18

REF. SHEET   5 A. HAZEBROUCK.   1/100,000

1. The 245th Machine Gun Company will move in the 150th Infantry Brigade Group from STEENVOORDE TO WESTBECOURT as under:-
   Transport on the 15th January 1918
   Personnel on the 16th January 1918.

2. The Transport with the exception of the marginally named will move by road on the 15th Jan 1918 to the RENESCURE staging area, and on the 16th Jan 1918 from there to WESTBECOURT.

TRANSPORT BY RAIL
3 1. L.G.S. WAGON
1 WATER CART
1 COOKS CART
5. L DR
4. Rg H
5

3. The marginally named vehicles and animals will proceed by rail from GODEWAERSVELDE to WIZERNES on the 16th Jan 1918.

4. The remainder of the Company will proceed by rail from GODEWAERSVELDE on the 16th Jan 1918 detraining at WIZERNE.

5. A lorry will arrive on the afternoon of the 15th Jan 1918 to carry Officers valises, Q.M. Stores and blankets to the station. The C.S.M. will detail a guard of 1 N.C.O & 2 men to accompany the lorry.

6. A rear party of 1 man will remain behind to take charge of area stores and hand over to incoming unit.

7. The 50th DIVISION will be in G.H.Q Reserve on arrival in the new area and will be ready to move by road or rail at 48 hours notice.

Copy no 1 File
"   " 2 Transport Officer
"   " 3 War Diary
"   " 4 War Diary

13. 1. 18.

(signed) Lieut
for Captain
Comdg 245th M.G. Coy.

SECRET. No 3.
APPx No 3.

245 MACHINE GUN COMPANY.

AFTER ORDER - REF OPERATION ORDER
No 32
13-1-18

2. Add:-
The Transport will start from Point
Q.1.C.1.3 at 9.30 AM. Jan 15th. 18.
Order for the 2nd day will be issued
at RENESCURE by B.T.O.
The following distances will be maintained
on the march.
Between units and Transport 100 yds.
A distance of 25 yards will be
maintained between every 6 Vehicles

W R Thom Capt.

14.1.18. for O.C. 245th M.G. Coy.

Copy No 1 File
" " 2 Transport Officer
" " 3 War Diary
" " 4 War Diary.

SECRET. App^x N° 4

50TH DIVISION OPERATION ORDER N° 161
24. JAN. 1918

1. The 50th Division (less Artillery) will relieve the 33rd Division (less Artillery) in the Right Sector of the Corps Front between January 27th and 30th.

2. The relief will take place in accordance with Table "B" attached.

3. The composition of Brigade Groups for the purposes of the relief will be:-

"A" Brigade Group.	"B" Brigade Group.	"C" Brigade Group.
149th Inf. Bde (less M.G. Company.)	150th Inf Bde (less M.G. Company).	50th Div. H.Q.
446th Field Coy R.E.	7th Field Coy R.E.	H.Q. & No1 Sect. Div Signal Coy.
1/3rd Nbn. Fld Amb.	2/2nd Nbn. Fld Amb.	151st Inf Bde (less M.G. Company).
H.Q. D.M.G.O.	7th D.L.I. (Pioneers)	447th Fld Coy R.E.
150th 151st M.G. Coys	No 4 Coy Div Train.	1/1st Nbn. Fld Amb.
No 2 Coy. Div Train.		149th & 245th M.G. Coys
		No 3 Coy Div Train

5. All troops of the 50th Division on detrainment at or east of BRANDHOEK will come under the orders of and be accommodated by the 33rd Division until the G.O.C. 50th Division takes over the Command of the Sector at 12 noon, January 30th.
They will be administered by the 50th Division.

6. Lewis and Vickers guns for Anti-Aircraft Defence will be taken over in accordance with Table "C" attached. The 7th D.L.I. (Pioneers) will so arrange their relief as to enable the 18th Middlesex Regt. (Pioneers) to proceed by the train detailed to take them to TILQUES.

7. All details of Defensive Arrangements, work in progress & proposed Defence Schemes, Aeroplane Photographs & special Maps will be taken over.

8. An advance party of 1 Officer and 16 O.R. per Brigade 33rd Division will arrive on the dates as shown below. They will be rationed and accommodated by Brigade.

January 25th	149th Infantry Brigade
January 27th	150th Infantry Brigade
January 27th	151st Infantry Brigade

11. Completion of moves to be reported by wire to 33rd Division and repeated to 50th Division.

15. G.O.C. 50th Division will assume command of the front at 12 noon Jan. 30th at which hour Divisional H.Q. will close at WIZERNES and open at YPRES.

18. Acknowledge.

(Sd). T A KENTISH. Capt G.S.
for Lt Col.
General Staff
50th Division.

Appendix "C" to 50th Div O.O no 161.

5. D.M.G.O will relieve Vickers Guns as follows.
   (a). 2 Posts of 2 guns each near HEINE HOUSE and AUGUSTUS WOOD, respectively.
   (b). 1 Gun in Vicinity of HAMBURG.
   (c). 1 Gun in Vicinity of BERLIN WOOD.
   (d). 1 Gun at each of Machine Gun Coy Camps in rear.

6. West of POTIJZE only 2 men per Lewis gun or Vickers Gun detailed for Anti-Aircraft Defence are required.

SECRET.   APP. No. 5

50TH DIVISION OPERATION ORDER No. 163
26TH JANUARY. 1918

1. The Machine Gun Companies of the 50th Division will relieve the Machine Gun Companies of the 33rd Division between the 27th & 30th Jan. 1918.

2. The 150th Machine Gun Company will relieve the 100th Machine Gun Company, and the 151st Machine Gun Company will relieve the 98th Machine Gun Company at "A" Echelon POTIJZE, on the morning of the 27th instant.

3. At dawn on the 28th instant the 151st Machine Gun Company will relieve the 19th Machine Gun Company in "A" Group positions in the line and the 150th Machine Gun Company will relieve the 248th Machine Gun Company in "B" Echelon Group position in the line. Details of relief to be arranged between Company Commanders concerned.

4. Tripods, Belt Boxes, S.A.A., Trench Stores, Maps, Battle orders, & Barrage sheets will be handed over on relief. Guns, spare parts, Etc, will be taken up into the line.

5. 50,000 rounds S.A.A. will be dumped by in the TILQUES area by each Machine Gun Company, and a similar amount will be taken over by each Machine Gun Company at POTIJZE Camp.

6. The 149th Machine Gun Company will relieve the 19th Machine Gun Company, & the 245th Machine Gun Company will relieve the 248th Machine Gun Company at "A" Echelon POTIJZE, on the morning of the 30th instant, & the 245th Machine Gun Company will become duty Company of the day.

7. Completion of relief to be wired in "B.A.B." Code to Brigade Headquarters in the line & to the D.M.G.O.

8. The Command of all Machine Guns in the area will pass to the D.M.G.O. 50th Division at 12 noon 30th instant.

9. Receipts will be obtained by all Companies of any stores, Etc, taken over from 33rd Division in the line & at POTIJZE Camp. Receipts to be handed in to Quartermaster's office as soon as possible.

10. Transport of 149th Machine Gun Company & 245th Machine Gun Company will proceed direct to POTIJZE Camp on 30th instant, unload & return direct to BRANDHOEK.

(sd). T. KENTISH Capt.
for G.S.O. 50th Division

Issued at 10.0 A.M.

245th MACHINE GUN COMPANY.

OPERATION ORDER No 33

Copy III

27th JAN. 1918.

REFCE 50th DIV. OP. ORDER No 161 d/ 24.1.18
- " - " 163 d/ 26.1.18
- " AD. INST. 27 d/ 24.1.18
MAPS Sheets 27 A. SE, 27, 28.
HAZEBROUCK. 5 A.

1. The 245th M.G. Coy will move in "C" Brigade Group from WESTBECOURT to "A" Echelon POTIJZE
   Transport on 29.1.18
   Personnel on 30.1.18

2. The Transport will move by road on the 29th as follows.
   WESTBECOURT - LUMBRES - SETQUES - WIZERNES - Xrds X 16 d 8.3 - Xrds X 10 d 4.8. starting Pt X.3.6.7.8.
   The starting point will be passed at 10.35 a.m. and the column joined.
   The Column will proceed to OUDEZEELE Staging Area, and on the 30th inst from there under orders of the B.T.O, to POTIJZE. After unloading it will return to BRANDHOEK.

3. The Remainder of the Company will proceed by rail from WIZERNES on the 30th inst detraining at YPRES.
   The march route will be WESTBECOURT - ACQUIN - LUMBRES - WIZERNES.
   Starting Point - Junction Road and Railway D.6 d.1.7 - to be passed at 8.2 A.M.
   2/Lt. LEE will report to the Brigade Major at WIZERNES station at 9.30 A.M. 30.1.18 and hand over the Company Entraining Strength.

4. A Lorry will arrive on the 29th inst to convey blankets, stores and Officer's Kits direct to POTIJZE on the 30th inst.
   A guard of 1 N.C.O and 3 men will accompany this lorry.

5. An advance party of 1 N.C.O. will report to the Entraining Officer at WIZERNES at 10 A.M. 28th inst and will proceed by No 2 train to BRANDHOEK.
   He will take rations for the 29th & 30th inst.

6. The 245th M.G. Coy will become duty Company of the day on arrival at "A" Echelon POTIJZE.

J.R. Houghton
Captain
O.C 245 M.G. Coy.

Copy 1. FILE
2. T.O.
3. WAR DIARY.
4. " "

SECRET.   APPX NO 7

50th DIVISION OPERATION ORDER No. 166.

31st January 1918.

1. The 149th Machine Gun Coy will relieve the 151st Machine Gun Coy in "A" Group, and the 245th Machine Gun Coy will relieve the 150th Machine Gun Coy in "B" Group on the night of 31st Jan/1st Feby 1918.

2. Guns and spare parts only will be taken in by the relieving Companies. All Tripods, Ammunition, Trench Stores, Maps and Photographs to be handed over.

3. All details of relief to be arranged between Company Commanders concerned.

4. Relief of "A" Group to be completed by dawn on 1st Feby.

5. Relief of "B" Group to be completed by 8.0 am on 1st Feby.

6. On completion of relief Capt. J. R. Houghton, 245th Machine Gun Coy, will assume command of all guns in "A" and "B" Groups.

7. Handing over certificates to be rendered to Quarter-Master's Office by 2.0 p.m. 1st prox.

8. Completion of relief to be wired in "B.A.B" French Code to Brigade Headquarters in the line and to D.M.G.O.

9. On relief 150th and 151st Machine Gun Companies will return to Nos 1 and 2 Camps, POTIJZE, respectively.

10. ACKNOWLEDGE.

(Signed) J. W. KENTISH.
Capt. G.S. for Lt. Col.
General Staff,
50th Division.

Issued at 7.30 am.

ORIGINAL

CONFIDENTIAL

WAR DIARY

OF

No 245 MACHINE GUN COMPANY

FROM FEBRUARY 1ST 1918 TO FEBRUARY 28TH

(VOLUME VII)

W R Thomson Capt
O.C 245 M G Coy

WAR DIARY or INTELLIGENCE SUMMARY

Army Form C. 2118.

(Erase heading not required.)

Place	Date	Hour	Summary of Events and Information	Remarks and references to Appendices
POT I J 2/5 I 3 d 2 5	4.2.18		Received 50th Division O.O no 169 from D.M.G.O	APPX N.o 1
			245 M.G. Coy in "B" Group relieving 151 M.G. Coy on the night 4/5th Feb.	APPX N.o 2
			Received 50th Division OO no 170 from D.M.G.O.	APPX N.o 3
	6.2.18		Received 50th Division OO no 171 from D.M.G.O.	APPX N.o 4
	7.2.18		245 M.G. Coy relieved no 150 M.G. Coy in "A" Group. 1.3 guns of 202 M.G. Coy 66th Division also "E" Batty (6 guns) & 1 gun BERLIN WOOD "B" Group	
	11.2.18		Received 50th Division OO no 173. from D.M.G.O	APPX N.o 5
	12.2.18		151st M.G. Coy relieved guns of 245 M.G. Coy in the Left Sector and 150th M.G. Coy relieved guns of 245 M.G. Coy in the Right Sector.	APPX N.o 6
	15.2.18		Received 50th Division OO no 176 from D.M.G.O. The 245th Machine Gun Company relieves the 150th Machine Gun Company in the Right Sector in the night of 16/17th Feb 18. No1 Section 1 gun from no 4 Section will relieve F1, F2 & F3 16/17th 2 Pdr 18. position no3 Section 3 guns from no 1 Section will relieve "A" & "C" Batteries position. L.T. GROVES will be in Command of "A" Battery, 2/Lt TEAGUE will be in Command of "C" Battery. no 2 Section will be attached to the Left Sector and according to order of O.O. 149. Machine Gun Company.	
			Received 50th Division OO no 178 from D.M.G.O	APPX N.o 9
	17.2.18 21.2.18		245 Machine Gun Company relieved in the line by no No 2 Coy, 33rd Division	APPX N.o 10
	22.2.18	7.30 am	Transport proceed by road on route for Acquin, halting for the night 22/23rd AT STEENVOORDE & the night 23/24th at RENESCURE. Company proceeded to WIZERNES by train entraining at YPRES, Ypres-ules by MARL TRACK from WIZERNES to ACQUIN	
		11 PM		

Army Form C. 2118.

WAR DIARY
or
INTELLIGENCE SUMMARY.

(Erase heading not required.)

Instructions regarding War Diaries and Intelligence Summaries are contained in F. S. Regs., Part II. and the Staff Manual respectively. Title pages will be prepared in manuscript.

Place	Date	Hour	Summary of Events and Information	Remarks and references to Appendices
ACQUIN 22.A.4.7 Sheet 27 A SE	22.2.18	8.30 pm	Company arrived at Acquin for training.	

L.R. Thomson Capt.
O.C. 245th M.G. Coy.

SECRET.

APPX N° 1

50TH DIVISION (MACHINE GUN) ORDER N° 169.

3RD FEB 1918.

1. The 150th Machine Gun Company will relieve the 149th Machine Gun Company in "A" Group, and the 151st Machine Gun Company will relieve the 245th Machine Gun Company in "B" Group on the night 4th/5th February 1918.

2. Guns & spare parts only will be taken in by the relieving Companies. All Tripods, Ammunition, Trench Stores, Maps, & photographs to be handed over.

3. All details of relief to be arranged between Company Commanders concerned.

4. Relief of "A" Group to be completed by dawn on 5th February.

5. Relief of "B" Group to be completed by 8 AM on 5th February.

6. On completion of relief Capt. D. Ralston. O.C. 151st Machine Gun Company will assume Command of all guns in "A" and "B" Groups.

7. Handing over certificates to be rendered to Quartermaster's Office by 2.0 p.m., 5th instant.

8. Completion of relief to be wired in "B.A.B." Trench code to Brigade Headquarters in the line & to D.M.G.O.

9. On relief the 149th & 245th Machine Gun Companies will return to Nos. 4. & 3 Camps POTIJZE respectively.

10. Acknowledge.

(Sgd). L.A. Kentish.
Capt. G.S. for Lt Col.
General Staff
50th Division

Issued at 5.0 p.m.

SECRET   APPx No 2.

RELIEF ORDERS   BY CAPTAIN. J.R. HOUGHTON.
O.C. M.G. GROUP IN THE LINE.

1. The 149th & 245th Machine Gun Companies will be relieved in "A" & "B" Groups respectively on the night of Feb. 4/5th 1918.

2. Lieut Mawson will issue RELIEF ORDERS for "A" Group. Relief of which will be completed by dawn 5/2/18.

3. GUIDES for "B" Group will be provided as follows. These guides with exception of guide for DAN Ho will be at HAMBURG at 5.45 A.M. on 5.2.18.
   GROUP HQ. DAN Ho one guide to be at junction of PLANK RD & MULE TK ZONNEBEKE STN at 5.15 A.M. 5.2.18
   BERLIN W.   1 guide provided by 2/LT PARSONS
   HAMBURG.   "   "   "   "   "   "
   "B" Batty. 1 Guide provided by LT. GRAVES.
   "C" "   "   "   "   " 2/LT DERBYSHIRE.

4. Guns & Spare parts only will be taken in by relieving teams. All tripods, S.A.A, Belt boxes Trench Stores, Maps, & defence Schemes etc will be handed over and receipt in triplicate obtained

5. O.C. "A" Group & officers i/c Battys of "B" Group will personally report relief complete & hand in handing over receipt to O.C. "A" Group at DAN. Ho.

6. Officers i/c Battys "B" Group will ensure that all empty Petrol tins and dirty socks are taken back to POTIJZE.

7. As soon as guns are loaded on to Pack mules at HAMBURG, sections will proceed independently under N.C.O's to Camp at POTIJZE

8. The Transport Officer 245 Coy will arrange for the following transport.
   1 MULE for 2 guns at DAN Ho to be at junction of PLANK RD & JUDAH TRACK at 5.45 A.M. 5.2.18.
   7 PACK ANIMALS for 14 guns to be at HAMBURG at 6.15 A.M. 5.2.18.

9. LT REES will arrange for a hot meal for relieved troops of 245 Coy to be provided at 7.15 A.M. 5.2.18.
   He will also arrange for baths for these N.C.O's & men as soon as possible.

issued at 2.30 pm.
3. 2. 18

(Sd) J.R. Houghton Capt.
O.C. M.G. Group

SECRET.
APPX No 2.

50TH DIVISION (MACHINE GUN) ORDER No 170.
3RD FEBY 1918.

1. The 50th Division will hand over front on the left and take over front on the Right, as detailed in 50th Division Operation Order no 167.

2. The D.M.G.O., 50th Division will make with the D.M.G.O. 66th Division the necessary arrangements for relieving the Machine Guns of the 66th Division in that part of the line which will be taken over.

3. The Relief will be carried out during the night of 8th/9th February.

4. Acknowledge. (D.M.G.O. & 66th Division only).

Issued at 5.0 pm.

(Sd). L.A.Kentish.
Capt G.S. for Lt. Col.
General Staff
50th Division.

SECRET   APPDX 4

50TH DIVISION (MACHINE GUN) ORDER. No 171.
6TH FEB. 1918

1. The 245th Machine Gun Coy will relieve the 150th Machine Gun Coy in "A" Group (less guns F.5. & F.6.) and 3 guns (nos 85, 86, & 87) of the 202nd Machine Gun Coy, 66th Division, also "E" Batty (6 guns) and 1 gun in BERLIN WOOD, "B" Group, on the 8th of February 1918.

2. During the afternoon of 8th February the 149th Machine Gun Company will relieve the 151st Machine Gun Coy in "B" Group (less "E" Batty & 1 gun in BERLIN WOOD). Also 2 guns ("B" Batty) 203rd Machine Gun Coy & 4 guns ("C" Batty) of the 202nd Machine Gun Coy, 66th Division.

3. The positions of guns F.5. & F.6 will be taken over by Lewis Gun Teams of 86th Infantry Brigade, 29th Division from the 150th Machine Gun Coy on the night 9th/10th February.

4. Guides & details of relief will be arranged between Company Commanders Concerned.

5. Relief of "A" Group will be completed by dawn on the 8th February.

6. Tripods, belt boxes, trench stores, maps & photographs to be handed over.

7. On Completion of relief Lieut P.H. HIGHT. O.C. 149 Machine Gun Coy will assume command of all guns in "A" & "B" Groups.

8. Handing over certificates to be rendered to Quartermaster's office by 9 p.m. 8th instant.

9. Completion of relief to be reported to in "B.AB" Trench Code to Brigade Headquarters in the line & to D.M.G.O.

10. On Relief the 150th & 151st Machine Gun Companies will return to Nos 1 & 2 Camps P0 & 15 25, respectively.

11. Acknowledge.

Issued at 8 p.m.

Signed L.A. Kentish
Capt. G.S. for Lt Col
General Staff
50th Division.

COMPANY OPERATION ORDER Nº 35.
By CAPTAIN J.R. HOUGHTON.
COMMANDING 245 M.G.Coy.

SECRET
APP. Nº 5
COPY Nº 10

Nº 245 Machine Gun Company will relieve certain gun positions of 150 & 151 M.G. Coys of the 50th Division & Nos 202 & 204 M.G. Coys of the 66th Division on the night of Feby 7/8th. & the afternoon of Feb 8th 1918. Two new gun positions in D.11.d.5.1. & D.11.d.5.3 will also be occupied.
The relief will be carried out as follows:-

Nº 2 SECTION. 2/LT ATTWATER

1 gun will relieve Nº 85 gun of 204 M.G. Coy. This gun will be known as F.1.
1 gun will relieve Nº 86 gun of 202 " . This gun will be known as F.2.
1 gun will relieve Nº 87 gun of " . This gun will be known as F.3.

Guns & spare parts only will be taken in.
Tripods, 14 belt boxes per gun, & all Trench Stores will be taken over.
1 Guide for each of these positions will be at Coy. H.Q. DEVIL'S CROSSING at 4.30 A.M. on the Morning of Feb 8th. Transport for these teams will go as far as the GASOMETERS - ZONNEBEKE.
Section H.Q. for these three guns will be established at present "B" Batty position (66th Division) This Batty will be Known as "A" Batty.

Nº 3 SECTION 2/LT TEAGUE

4 guns will relieve F.1, F.3, F.4, C.1 of 150 M.G. Coy
These guns will be known as F.4, F.5, F.6 & S.3.
2 guns will occupy positions at D.11.d.5.1. & D.11.d.5.3. old Rt. Section H.Q. These guns will be Known as S.1 & S.2
4 guides for 4 guns of 150 Coy will be at HAMBURG at 4.30 A.M. on the Morning of Feb 8th.
Guns only will be taken in for these positions
Belt boxes, S.A.A. Tripods, Trench Stores will be taken over.
S1. & S.2 positions. Guns Tripods, & 14 belt boxes per gun will be taken in. 5 boxes S.A.A. & 12 very lights for each position will be drawn from SEINE DUMP.
Section H.Q. for these 6 guns will be at present Rt forward section H.Q. S.1 & S.2 will be in position by dawn 8.2.18.

Nº 4 SECTION. 2/LT DERBYSHIRE

"B" Batty AUGUSTUS WOOD. will be relieved by 6 guns This Batty will be Known as "E" Batty.
1 Guide for this Batty will be provided by 151 M.G. Coy. at 5.30 p.m. on the afternoon of the 8th Feb. 1918.
4 Tripods, all belt boxes, S.A.A. & Trench Stores will be taken over.
6 guns & 2 Tripods & spare parts for 6 guns will be taken in.
1 Team will relieve one team of 151 Coy at BERLIN WOOD This will be Known as R.1. 1 Gun, Tripod belt boxes S.A.A. will be taken over from 151 M.G. Coy.
The one gun at BERLIN WOOD will be relieved at 4.30 p.m. 8th Feb 18. No guides will be required for this gun.
Lt. Rew will be in Command of all 245 M.G. Coy guns in the line, he will establish his HQ at HEINE HQ

Issued at 7.30 p.m.
6.2.18

J R Houghton Captain
O.C. 245 M.G. Coy

SECRET. APP: No. 6.

50TH DIVISION (MACHINE GUN) ORDER No. 173.
11TH FEB. 1918.

1. The following Machine Gun relief will take place on 12th February 1918.
The 150th Machine Gun Company (less one Section) will take over F.1.2.3 positions and A, B and C Batteries. The 151st Machine Gun Company (plus remaining section of 150 Machine Gun Company) will take over F.4.5.6.7.8.9., S.1.2.3.4. positions and D. E. and F. Batteries.

2. Guns & spare parts only will be taken in by relieving Companies. All Tripods, Ammunition, Trench stores, Maps & Photographs to be handed over.

3. All details of relief to be arranged between Company Commanders concerned.

4. Relief of "Forward Guns" to be completed by 7 pm. 12th instant.

5. Relief of "Batteries" to be completed by 6 pm. 12th instant.

6. Revised Defence Scheme will come into force at 6 pm. 12th instant. Incoming Battery Commanders are responsible that the new barrage lines are laid out and the Battery positions correctly marked previous to that hour.

7. The 151st & 150th Machine Gun Companies Headquarters will be established at TYNE COTS. and DEVIL'S CROSSING respectively.

8. Handing over certificates to be rendered to Quartermasters Office by 2 pm. 13th instant.

9. Completion of relief to be wired in "BAB" Trench Code to Brigades in the line and to D.M.G.O.

10. On relief the 149th & 245th Machine Gun Companies will return to Nos 4 & 3 Camps. POTIJZE, respectively.

11. Acknowledge.

Issued at 5 pm.

Signed E C Ausley
Lt Col.
General Staff
50th Division.

SECRET.
APPX No 7.

OPERATION ORDERS No 36. ISSUED BY
CAPTAIN J.R. HOUGHTON.
COMMANDING 245TH MACHINE GUN COMPANY.

The 245th Machine Gun Company will be relieved by the 150th & 151st Machine Gun Companies on Feb. 12th 18.

The 151st Machine Gun Company will relieve guns of 245th Machine Gun Company in the Left Sector.

The 150th Machine Gun Company will relieve guns in Right Sector F.1. F.2. F.3.

The gun in BERLIN WOOD. S.4. will be handed over to relieving team of 151st M.G. Coy.

All other guns — 12 in all will be brought. In addition one Tripod, will be brought out by No 3 Section.

GUIDES. No 3 Section will provide the following guides to be at HAMBURG at 6pm. on 12.2.18.

1 guide for F.4 & 5. — old S.1 & S.2.
1 "   each for F.6. 7. 8. & 9.

No 4 Section will provide 1 guide for BERLIN WOOD. S.4. at HAMBURG at 4 p.m.

6 guns at AUGUSTUS WOOD. will be withdrawn at 6pm.

H.Q. HEINE. Ho. will be withdrawn on completion of relief of gun teams.

Relief complete to be reported to TYNE COT.

LT. HIGHT. will arrange relief of F.1. F.2. & F.3.

TRANSPORT. T.O. 245 Coy will arrange for the following Transport.

Transport for 6 guns from AUGUSTUS WOOD. to be at HAMBURG at 6pm.

Transport for 6 guns and 1 tripod to be at HAMBURG at 7.15 p.m. Feb 12th 18.

All petrol tins and dirty sacks will be brought out by Nos. 2. 3. & 4 Sections.

W.R. Thomson
Captain
O.C. 245 M.G. Coy.

Issued at 6pm.
11. 2. 18.

SECRET   APP. N° 8

50TH DIVISION (MACHINE GUN) ORDER N° 176.

15TH FEB. 18.

1. The following Machine Gun relief will take place on the night of the 16/17th Feb. 18. The 245th Machine Gun Company (less one section) will take over F.1. F.2. F.3 positions and A. B. & C Batteries from the 150th Machine Gun Company. The 149th Machine Gun Company (plus remaining section of the 245th Machine Gun Company) will take over F.4. 5. 6. 7. 8. 9. S.1. 2. 3. 4. positions and D. E. & F Batteries from the 151st Machine Gun Company.

2. Guns spare parts only will be taken in by the relieving Companies. All Tripods, Ammunition, Trench Stores, Maps & Photographs to be handed over.

3. All details of relief to be arranged between Company Commanders concerned.

4. Relief of "Forward Guns" to be completed by dawn 17th instant.

5. Relief of "Batteries" to be completed by 8 A.M. 17th instant.

6. The 149th & 245th Machine Gun Companies Headquarters will be established at TYNE COTS and DEVILS CROSSING respectively.

7. Handing over certificates to be rendered to Quartermasters Office by 2.0 p.m. 17th instant.

8. Completion of relief to be wired in "B.A.B" Trench Code to Brigades in the line and to D.M.G.O.

9. On Relief the 150th & 151st Machine Gun Companies will return to Nos 1. & 2 Camps POTIJZE, respectively.

10. Acknowledge.

(Signed) E. C. Austey.
Lt Col.
General Staff
50th Division

Issued at. 4 pm.

OPERATION ORDER No 37.
ISSUED BY CAPTAIN J.R. HOUGHTON
COMMANDING 245 MACHINE GUN COMPANY

App. No 9 SECRET
Copy No 8

1. The 245th Machine Gun Company less 1 Section will relieve the 150th Machine Gun Company in the Right Sector on the night of 16/17th Feby 1918.
   Relief of forward guns to be complete by dawn Feb. 17th.
   Relief of Barrage guns to be complete by 8. A.m. Feb. 17th.

2. No 1 Section & 1 gun from No 4 Section will relieve F.1 F.2 F.3 and "B" Battery positions
   No 3 Section & 3 guns from No 4 Section will relieve A & C Battery positions.
   LT. GRAVES will be in command of "A" Batty.
   2/LT. TEAGUE will be in command of "C" Batty.
   No 2 Section will be attached to the left Sector and will act according to orders of O.C. 149 M.G. Coy.

3. Guns & spare parts only will be taken in by relieving teams.
   All tripods, belt boxes, S.A.A. and trench stores will be taken over.

4. Guides will be provided by 150 M.G Coy as follows:-
   F.1. F.2. F.3. - one guide for each at DEVIL'S CROSSING AT 5.0 A.M. Feb 17th 18
   A & B. Batteries - 1 guide each at DEVIL'S CROSSING. AT 5.0 A.M. 17.2.18
   Limbers will be unloaded at the GASOMETERS ZONNEBEKE.
   C. Batty 1 guide will be at the junction of JUDAH TRACK and the PLANK ROAD. at 5.0 A.M.
   Transport will be taken to this point

5. T.O. 245 M.G. Coy will arrange for necessary transport.

6. Acknowledge

Issued at
15.2.18

J R Houghton
Captain
O.C. 245 M.G. Coy.

Copies 1. D.M.G.O.
2. O.C. 150 M.G. Coy.
3. O.C. 149 M.G. Coy.
4. T.O. 245 M.G. Coy.
5.6.7 Section Officers
8.9. War Diary.

SECRET. APP.No. 10

50TH DIVISION (MACHINE GUN) ORDER No 178.
17TH FEB. 1918.

1. In accordance with 50th Division Operation Order No 175, the 50th Division Machine Gun Companies will be relieved in the line by the 33rd Division Machine Gun Companies on the 20th and 21st in accordance with attached Table "A".

2. No 3 Company, 33 Division will relieve 245th Machine Gun Company in F.1. 2. 3. positions and A, B, C, Batteries.
   No 2 Company, 33rd Division will relieve 149th Machine Gun Company in F 4. 5. 6, 7 & 9., S. 1. 2. 3. 4 positions and D. E. and F. Batteries.

3. Guns spare parts only will be taken in by the relieving Companies. All tripods, Ammunition, Trench Stores, Maps & Photographs to be handed over.

4. All details of relief to be arranged between Company Commanders concerned.

5. Relief of "Forward guns" to be completed by Noon 21st instant.

6. Relief of "Rear guns" to be completed by 7.0 A.m. 21st instant.

7. Handing over certificates to be tendered to Quartermaster's Office by 8.0 A.M. 21st instant.

8. Completion of relief to be wired in "BAB" Trench Code to Brigades in the line and to D. M. G. O.

9. The 150th & 151st Machine Gun Companies less transport will move to the new area on the 26th instant under orders to be issued by the 151st Brigade Group.

10. Headquarters, 149th & 245th Machine Gun Companies (less transport) will move to the new area on 22nd instant. under orders to be issued by the 150th Brigade Group.

11. On arrival in the new Area the Machine Gun Companies will again come under the orders of the D. M. G. O.

12. Transport will move according to attached Table "A".

13. Attention is directed to paras. 4. 5. 6. 7. 9. 50th Division Administrative Instructions No 31.

14. On Completion of relief the D. M. G. O. 33rd Division will take over Command of all Machine Guns in the line. The D. M. G. O's Office will close at 9 A.M. 24th instant & will open at West Becourt at the same time (Sd) E. Audley Lt Col

15. Acknowledge.

50th Divisional Troops

BECAME "D" COMPANY 50th MACHINE GUN BATTALION

245th MACHINE GUN COMPANY

MARCH 1918

War Diary of "D" Coy for March 1919.

Army Form C.2118.

Sheet 1.

WAR DIARY
INTELLIGENCE SUMMARY.
(Erase heading not required.)

Place	Date	Hour	Summary of Events and Information	Remarks and references to Appendices
ACQUIN. 22.A.4.Y. SHEET 27A SE.	1.3.18		Received 179th Infantry Brigade Warning Order No 243. Bourdon to be prepared to move at 24 hours notice.	Appx 1
	8.3.18		Received 149th Infantry Brigade Operation Order No 244 & Warning order No 243 dated 28.2.18 with the result the operation today 8th March.	Appx 2
		2.10 PM	Company proceeded by Mechanical Route to ST. OMER, on route for BLANGY-TRONVILLE, entraining at ST OMER at 9.50 & detraining at MOREUIL at 10 a.m. 9.3.18 & proceeded by march Route to BLANGY-TRONVILLE.	Appx 3
BLANGY-TRONVILLE SHEET 17 A10C5.2	10.3.18		Received Verbal Warning from D.M.G.O. 9th Corps that Company would move by march route from BLANGY-TRONVILLE to VAUVILLERS.	Appx 4
VAUVILLERS SHEET 17 A19C5/2	11.3.18		In billets at VAUVILLERS with M.G. Battalion H.Q.	
	12 "		Received 50th Div. W.O. No 182 - Repaired in Coy. W.O. No 39. Reconnoitred Routes to GUILLAUCOURT & ROZIÈRES.	Appx 5
	13 "		Received 50th Div. W.O. No 183 concerning obstruction of the Division on the FIFTH ARMY front in case of a hostile attack succeeding against our front - Issued Coy. W.O. No 40.	Appx 6
	15 "		Informed at Conference of MG Coy Commanders under the Commanding Officer of the 50th Batt M.G.C. (Lt. Col. HARPER M.C.) that Div. W.O. No 183 would be altered. The Div. would proceed to FINS to Counter attack & Capture either the village of METZ-EN-COUTURE or NEUVILLE-BOURJONAL (Ref: Sheet 57 C S.E. 1/20,000 & VALENCIENNES Sheet 12 1/100,000). All objectives were given to the M.G. Coys attached their various tasks. A plan of the ground was constructed at HARGONNIÈRES by the 7th D.L.I. & this was studied by all concerned.	
	19 "		Proceeded with the Section Officers concerned Lt. GRAVES No 3 Sn. & 2/Lt DERBYSHIRE No 4 Sn by motor lorry with representatives of other M.G. Coy's to reconnoitre the ground at METZ-EN-COUTURE. Fixed all guns & issued Maps of operation.	Appx 7.
	20 "		All Coy. preparing for the Counter attack - all men who were to be engaged were taken by their Section Officers to see the plan of the ground. Received Tactical Instructions No 1 50th MG Bn. Issued Tactical Instructions No 1.	Appx 7A

Army Form C. 2118.

Sheet 2.

WAR DIARY
or
INTELLIGENCE SUMMARY.

(Erase heading not required.)

Instructions regarding War Diaries and Intelligence Summaries are contained in F. S. Regs., Part II. and the Staff Manual respectively. Title pages will be prepared in manuscript.

Place	Date	Hour	Summary of Events and Information	Remarks and references to Appendices
VAUVILLERS (Ref^a AMIENS 17)	21st	9AM	Received wire M77 from Battⁿ - read out to all concerned	App^x 8
		10AM	Received wire MG F2 from Battⁿ - on 4 hours notice for moving from billets to entraining stations.	
		3.20pm	Received verbal orders from C.O. to move at once - train leaving GUILLAUCOURT 5pm. with 151st Inf. Bde Group. No orders as to destination.	
		5pm	Moved by march route from VAUVILLERS with personnel to GUILLAUCOURT.	
		6pm	Entrained (Transport moved by road at 4.30pm staging for night at VILLERS - CARBONNEL under 151st Bde. T.O.).	
Ref^a Sheet 62 C 1/40,000.		10.15am	Arrived BRIE - UNHOUND. Received orders from B.G.C. 151st Inf Bde. to proceed by march route to BEAUMETZ & bivouac for night in field. Divⁿ HQ to b at BEAUMETZ	
		11pm	Moved by march route via MESNIL-BRUNTEL & CARTIGNY to a field 1/4 mile N.W. of BEAUMETZ.	
ST. QUENTIN Sheet 18 1/100,000 BEAUMETZ	22nd	2AM	Bivouacked for night in open field.	
		6AM	Lt. REES conducted party to hutc at Divⁿ HQ. ordered by C.O. to be prepared to take up positions as soon as transport arrived. C.O. gave us area in 2 behind the Green Line, which was; BOUCLY - BERNES - BOUILLY - CAULAINCOURT - BEAUVOIS - VAUX with a second Switch line; HANCOURT - VRAIGNES - MONCHYLAGACHE - CROIX MOLIGNAUX - CANAL. Posn to be reconnoitred at BOUCLY to prevent enemy advance down COLOGNE RIVER Bed.	App^x 9
		11AM	Proceeded with Lt. GRAVES & 2/Lt. DERBYSHIRE to BOUCLY to find position. Enemy captured ROISEL.	
		2PM	Transport arrived. Ordered nos 3 & 4 Sun. to take up posn at BOUCLY.	
		4PM	8 guns in posn. Received verbal orders from C.O. to withdraw guns from BOUCLY as Green line was being hard pressed at VRAIGNES. Returned to BEAUMETZ & awaited orders at Divⁿ H.Q.	
		10pm	Received orders from C.O. to withdraw from BEAUMETZ by road. Transport Nos 1 & 2 Sun. to CARTIGNY, Coy H.Q., No 3 & 4 Sun. to ST. CREN.	

Army Form C. 2118.
Sheet 3.

WAR DIARY
or
INTELLIGENCE SUMMARY.
(Erase heading not required.)

Place	Date	Hour	Summary of Events and Information	Remarks and references to Appendices
BEAUMETZ	Dec 23rd	11 pm	Withdrew in accordance with orders (MG Bde) to ST. CREN	
ST. CREN		2 AM	Arrived ST. CREN. ½ Coy. Slept in Langs Stable. – Transport & both ½ Coy. at CARTIGNY. Rest returned. Commenced. Appendix 10 Map Shows Routes & Places for the movement.	App 10
		6 AM	Col Hunter issued verbal orders for positions to be taken up in trench lines across BRIE – MONS-EN-CHAUSSÉE Road at O.29 Ref. Sht 62c 1/40,000.	
		6.20 AM	Moved 2 sections by march route to trench line	
		10.15 AM	8 guns in position to check enemy advance along main road onto Bridge over Canal at BRIE. Depress under BGC. 150th Inf. Bde. Orders when orders the guns were fired. No Infantry on right of road when Mr. DERBYSHIRE had 4 guns. ½ Coy. on left of road in trench. When Lt. GRAVES had 4 guns. Orders given to the guns to conform with the Infantry in retiring. Positions to be taken up further back until over the BRIE Bridge. Meanwhile Lt. REES with the Transport & No. 1 & 2 gn. (Mr. PARSONS, Mr. ATTWATER & Mr. TEAGUE with Mr. SEAMOUR ½ Transport) had to wait across the Bridges. The 8 guns being placed in positions along the W. Bank of the Canal to defend the crossing.	Apps 11
		10.30 AM	Action Commenced Germans advancing Widely over distant ridges along main road and on both flanks.	
		12 noon	All guns in action – ranges varying from 500 to 2500 yds. Enemy everywhere movement on right flank. Mr. DERBYSHIRE retired to better positions to guard this flank. Caused considerable casualties. Lt. GRAVES with 4 guns seat off to attack.	
		3 pm	Commenced actual retirement along the main road BRIE. Lightly shelled. Maintainfire in co. from Co. Bumpf filled on left of road & pour returning	

Army Form C. 2118.

Sheet 4.

WAR DIARY
or
INTELLIGENCE SUMMARY.
(Erase heading not required.)

Place	Date	Hour	Summary of Events and Information	Remarks and references to Appendices
BRIE Ref. 62C 1/40,000 & AMIENS 17 1/100,000.	23rd	3.50 p.m.	6 guns out of 8 safely across BRIE Bridge. 2 put out of action – 4 men wounded enemy paying particular attention to our carrying guns.	
		4 p.m.	Bridge blown up. Heavy fire opened by Artillery & M.G.s under Lt. Rees on W. bank of canal to stop enemy behind the ridge E. of BRIE & prevent direct observation on the abnormal movement of transport & troops up the main road to VILLERS-CARBONNEL. Enemy aeroplanes exclusively active all day flying very low observing defences & firing at any movement. Did no damage whatever.	
Ref. 62C N.33.b.		5 p.m.	Collected Nos 3 & 4 Guns & proceeded via VILLERS-CARBONNEL under cover from Col. Harper to Transport lines on small road leading from main ESTRÉES – VILLERS-CARBONNEL road southwards to BERNY-EN-SANTERRE – 100x from main road.	
		7 p.m.	Nearly killed – moved Transport & personnel further South towards BERNY – her in trench system. Received note from Lt. REES at BRIE Bridge that Lt. ATTWATER had been killed – they were being heavily shelled, but expected relief at dawn.	
	24th	8 A.M.	Moved Nos 3 & 4 Gun Unit Transport by march route to CHAULNES via GENERMONT & ABLAINCOURT – Transport via VERMANDOVILLERS. Col. Harper sent D.R. to CHAULNES to order us to return to FOUCAUCOURT but he missed the Coy. on the crowded roads.	
CHAULNES		12 noon	Halted for 1 hour. But could find no trace of 50th Divn. decided to strike the AMIENS–ST QUENTIN Road at RAINECOURT. Transport under Lt. DERBYSHIRE turned back by D.R. & joined M.G. Battn at FOUCAUCOURT at 3 p.m. Moved Nos 3 & 4 Guns by road via HERLEVILLE to FOUCAUCOURT.	
FOUCAUCOURT		6 p.m.	Down 25th at BRIE Bridge. ½ Coy. to be relieved at ½ Coy. Transport at M.G. Battn. Remaining ½ Coy. to be relieved at Church. Returned to FOUCAUCOURT.	

4

WAR DIARY or INTELLIGENCE SUMMARY.

Army Form C. 2118.
Sheet 5

Place	Date	Hour	Summary of Events and Information	Remarks and references to Appendices
FOUCAUCOURT (62 C 40000 & AMIENS 1)	25th	4 AM	Lt. REES with remaining ½ Coy. (Nos. 1 & 2 Sec.) withdrew without rail. from the line at BRIE Bridge under orders from 8th Divn. arriving FOUCAUCOURT 10 AM	
		10 AM	All Coy. & Transport with 14 guns complete. Received 2 more M.G.'s from Batt.	
		6 p.m.	Received orders to prepare to move.	
		8 p.m.	Moved by march route to Divn. H.Q. 1½ miles W. of FOUCAUCOURT. Enemy across the Canal at ST. CHRIST & PARGNY & advancing on CHAULNES	
	26th	3 AM	Moved by march route via FRAMERVILLE to VAUVILLERS arriving 5-30 AM. Placed men in old billets. Awaited arrival of Batt. Harpur.	
VAUVILLERS		8 AM	Got. Harpur informed us that a trench line (under preparation by R.E.'s) was to be held running FRAMERVILLE - VAUVILLERS - ROSIÈRES to be held by 12 M.G.'s of the Coy. Reconnoitred positions & Sect. Officers Lt. GRAVES, Lt. TEAGUE & 2nd Lt. DERBYSHIRE occupied posts in the line at 10 A.M. Established Coy. H.Q. at light Rly. Stn. at junction of VAUVILLERS - HARBONNIÈRES road with RIHONS - HARBONNIÈRES road. Placed No. 1 Sect. (Mr. PARSONS) in position on light Railway 300° N. of road junction to protect left of line from FRAMERVILLE direction. See map.	App. 7. 12
			Bn. H.Q. near Coy. H.Q. Divn. H.Q. in HARBONNIÈRES.	
		2 p.m.	Germans attacked FRAMERVILLE & our troops withdrew; counter attacked & again recaptured it. Fairly quiet night but locality of enemy uncertain.	
		6 p.m.	Bde. H.Q. moved back to HARBONNIÈRES. Moved Coy. H.Q. to keep in touch to same town. Notified Sect. Officers & established Report posts at old Coy. H.Q.	
HARBONNIÈRES	27th	5 AM	Enemy bearing behind woods running N. from LIHONS. Enemy reported fired on by all guns but no actual attack made. Enemy concentrations dispersed by Artillery fire.	

WAR DIARY or INTELLIGENCE SUMMARY

Place	Date	Hour	Summary of Events and Information	Remarks and references to Appendices
HARBONNIÈRES	27"	6 p.m.	Enemy attacked VAUVILLERS - ROSIÈRES line & 2/party with Robins. 4/Lt. DERBYSHIRE & 2/Lt. TEAGUE withdrew later & reported for orders. 2nd GRAVES manned at ROSIÈRES with MG. Dism. ordered 4/Lt. DERBYSHIRE to take up from line his 4 guns at the road junction firing on VAUVILLERS. 2/Lt. TEAGUE on ROSIÈRES - GUILLAUCOURT Railway firing in VAUVILLERS direction. N°3 Sec'n withdrawn under orders from G.L. Harper to HARBONNIÈRES. Line now	
		8 p.m.	approximately along light railway from foot N. of road junction to ROSIÈRES. Enemy in FRAMERVILLE, VAUVILLERS & E. of ROSIÈRES. 3 advancing W. along ground N. of AMIENS - ST. QUENTIN Road from PROYART.	
	28"	3 a.m.	Division in danger of being cut off in rear by enemy advance S. onto BAYONVILLERS & GUILLAUCOURT. General movement ordered onto a line along the railway ROSIÈRES - GUILLAUCOURT.	
CAIX		7 a.m.	Movement onto new line successfully carried out. N°. 1, 3 & 4 Sec'ns with Coy. H.Q. moved by track route via HARBONNIÈRES across the Railway to CAIX. Coy. H.Q. established in Sunken Road ¼ mile N.W. of village.	
		8 a.m.	G.L. Harper ordered me to place 8 guns in pos'n in wood on CAIX - GUILLAUCOURT Road ½ way between the 2 villages. Detailed 4/Lt. PARSONS (N°s 1 & 4) & 4/Lt. DERBYSHIRE (N°s 4 & 3) to occupy this posn.	
		10 a.m.	8 guns in pos'n fired immediately after by Lt. GRAVES & 2/Lt. TEAGUE with 4 guns. Enemy commenced attack along railway line GUILLAUCOURT - ROSIÈRES succeeding in places. Counter attacks drove him back in these places but the advance could be hold by M.G. Enemy holding wood & crest ½ miles E. & N.E. of CAIX - GUILLAUCOURT Road opposite wood held by 12 guns of 16 Coy.	

WAR DIARY or INTELLIGENCE SUMMARY

Army Form C.2118.

Sheet 7.

Place	Date	Hour	Summary of Events and Information	Remarks and references to Appendices
CAIX (AMIENS 17 1/100,000)	28?	11 AM	Organized Coy. M.G., No. 3 Sect. & Infantry stragglers into Platoon with 4 Lewis guns & took up position to E. edge of wood in N. of CAIX - CAYEUX Road to cover retirement of our 12 guns from the wood which the enemy were now strongly attacking. Ammunition gave out in "K" Wood at 1 pm & a withdrawal to CAIX was ordered. The 3 Sectn under Lt. GRAVES carrying guns & tripods retired via CAIX, BEAUCOURT, MEZIÈRES, MOREUIL to ROUVREL arriving 10 pm.	
		1 pm	Coy. M.G. & No. 3 Sect. of an Infantry Batt. covering fire to the above retirement to the wood out of the wood onto the N. edge of CAIX-CAYEUX Rd. between this wood & CAYEUX. From this position fire was given during several attacks by the enemy against 39° Divn. from direction of WIENCOURT. Covering fire was given for two counter-attacks - the first succeeding in driving the enemy back into WIENCOURT.	
		5 pm	Coy. Harper ordered withdrawal of these troops to IGNAUCOURT via CAYEUX - both of which villages were being shelled by gun artillery.	
IGNAUCOURT		8 pm	In absence of further orders (Capt. MCPHAIL) through our own lines when near MARCELCAVE - IGNAUCOURT - BEAUCOURT. Had our [?] point be covered by 66th Divt. Reached DEMUIN at	
DEMUIN	29°	8 am	10 pm & put him under cover as it was raining heavily. Moved by march route to HANGARD where he met Col. Harper who ordered to proceed to DOMART & establish Coy. H.Q.	
DOMART.		10 AM	Arrived DOMART-SUR-LA-LUCE & put Coy. under cover. Established Coy. H.Q. and Collected & rationed all Infantry & M.G's. Sent them up into LIRAGES to Divn. Area in the line 570 S.S. Divn in Civil. Support to 207. LTD. ½ mile S. of DEMUIN.	

Army Form C. 2118.

Sheet 8.

WAR DIARY
or
INTELLIGENCE SUMMARY.
(Erase heading not required.)

Place	Date	Hour	Summary of Events and Information	Remarks and references to Appendices
DOMART (AMIENS 17)	29°	9 AM	3 Sectn under Lt. GRAVES moved by march route from ROUVREL to BOVES following M.G. Batt. Transport & details in billets.	
		3 PM	Co., Hanson gave orders for all details of Coy. to be handed to BOVES in order that the Coy. might be re-organised for further fighting. Moved by road to BOVES arriving 6 p.m. & joining remainder of Coy. & Transport. 245 Coy. now altogether at BOVES.	
BOVES	30"	6 p.m		
		8 PM	Received 102° Div. O.X.F.028 for move & concentration of Transports & Details of Coy. O.O. No. 41. Bn. List transport to SAINS-EN-AMIENOIS. Issued Coy. O.O. No. 41.	App. 13
		9.30 PM	Moved with Transport by march route to SAINS-EN-AMIENOIS arriving 12 noon. All men in billets - room full of French troops, weather constantly bad	
SAINS-EN-AMIENOIS		1 p.m	Total casualties for operations from 22nd to date 20 officers killed (Capt. LYONS Capt. - 2/Lt. E ATTWATER HOUGHTON, SIMMS Lieut 44 M.G. Coy. but on strength ((C.S.M.), 9 O.R 3 O.R. killed (including 2 Corpls.), 1 W.O. Wounded (1 Sgt., 1 Cpl.), 7 men missing. Wounded (including animals 7 mules & 4 L.D. horses killed 2½ limbers missing.	
	31st	10 AM	Received XIX Corps Administrative Instructions App #14 & 50° Div. W.O. No. 190 App #14 & 50° Div. W.O. No. 1 - Issued Coy. W.O. No. 42 for move to SALEUX & Lift 150° Inf. Bde. W.O. No. 1 - Issued Coy. W.O. No. 42 for move to SALEUX & entrained to RUE. Transport moved lift 150° Bde. transport at 12.30 p.m.	App #15
		3 p.m	Staging the night at BOURDON. Received verbal instructions from Battn. H.Q. to get to SALEUX as soon as possible as train would leave at 5 p.m. Arrived SALEUX with Coy/Bn. transport (3) at 4.30 p.m. No clear instructions being obtainable for midnight. Men under cover in large shed by Station. We kept	

L.R.Thomson Capt. OC 245 M.G. Coy.

(Copy) SECRET

149TH INFANTRY BRIGADE WARNING ORDER No. 243

Ref. Map 1/20,000.
Sheet 27 A. S.E.
28TH FEB. 1918

1. The 50th Division while in the TILQUES Training area is in G.H.Q. Reserve and is under orders to be prepared to move at 24 hours notice.

2. In the event of the Division being ordered to entrain at short notice the 149th Inf. Bde. Group will comprise the following units:
   - 149th Inf. Bde.
   - 2 M.G. Companies
   - 7th Field Co. R.E.
   - 13rd N'bn. Fd. Ambce.
   - No 2 Coy Div. Train.
   - H.Q. Divisional Train
   - 244 Div. Employment Co.
   - 1st N'bn. Mob. Vet. Section.

3. In the event of entrainment being ordered the 149th Inf. Bde. Group will entrain at ST. OMER, in accordance with the attached table. The times of departure of trains and times for the respective units to pass their starting point will be notified to units if an entrainment is ordered.

4. All units will have their route according to the attached table including the approaches into the Railway Station carefully reconnoitred by the necessary number of Officers N.C.O's who may be required to guide their units either by day or night.

5. (a). The 5th North'd Fusiliers will be prepared to send Serial No 18 (1 Coy, 1 Cooker, 1 Team) to act as loading party for the Brigade Group.

   (b). Serial No 4 (1 Coy, 1 Cooker and Team of 4th North'd Fus'rs) will in the event of a move act as unloading party for the Brigade Group on arrival at the detraining station.

6. The 5th North'd Fusiliers will detail a Senior officer to act as entraining officer at ST. OMER. This officer will reconnoitre the railway approaches & accommodation & be prepared to take up his duties immediately on receipt of orders.

   The 4th North'd Fusiliers will detail a Senior officer to travel on No 1 Train to act as detraining officer.

Sgd W. Anderson
Capt.
Brigade Major
149th Infantry Bde.

Issued at 5.0. P.M.

(Copy) SECRET.

149TH INFANTRY BRIGADE OPERATION ORDER No. 244
8TH MARCH 1918.

1. The 149th Inf Bde Warning Order No 243 dated 28th February 1918, will be put into operation today 8th March.

2. Entraining Station for Brigade Group --- ST OMER.
   Detraining Station for Brigade Group --- MOREUIL.

3. (a) All units except Infantry will arrive complete at entraining station three hours before the time of departure of their train.
   Transport of Infantry Battalions will arrive at entraining station three hours before time of departure of their train.
   Infantry personnel will arrive at entraining station 1½ hours before time of departure of train.
   (b) Para. 5 of warning order is cancelled.
   Infantry Battalions will detail their own loading party, strength 1 officer & 50 O.R. who will also unload at detraining station.
   All other units will be responsible for their own loading & unloading, under specially detailed officers.

4. (a) Units will pass their respective starting points as shown in Table A. attached.
   (b) The times of departure of trains are as shown in Table A. attached.

5. Captain GRIFLING, 5th N.F. will act as entraining officer at ST. OMER.
   Captain FINLAYSON, 4th N.F. will act as detraining officer at MOREUIL.

6. Baggage supply wagons will accompany units to which they are allotted.

7. Entraining of units must be completed ½ hour before time of departure of train.

8. Senior Officer on each train will be in command of the train & will detail picquets for each end of the train at all stops to prevent troops leaving.

9. Water bottles must be carried full.

10. Arrangements will be made by units for the watering of horses before entraining, & also at hours laid at TAINQUES if R.T.O. there reports to O.C. train that there is time.

11. Advance parties consisting of the Staff Captain, and 1 officer & 2 O.R's per unit with bicycles, who will entrain two trains earlier than their units, who report to Admin Commandant, VILLERS BRETONNEUX for instructions. They will meet their units on detraining & act as guides.

12. Brigade HQ. will close at BOISDINGHEM at 12 noon 8th Mch.

Sgd W. Anderson
Capt.
Issued at 10.0 am 149th Inf Brigade Major.

SECRET

OPERATION ORDER No 37 BY CAPTAIN W.R. THOMSON
COMMANDING 245 MACHINE GUN COY.

REFCE. 27A SE 1/20,000
AMIENS 17. 1/100,000

LE NOOVRE.
8TH MARCH. 1918

1. 245 Machine Gun Coy will move with the 149th Inf. Bde Group from LE NOOVRE to BLANGY TRONVILLE on 8th inst.

2. The Coy will move by march route to ST. OMER parading outside Coy. H.Q. in column of four facing ACQUIN at 2.10 P.M. Starting point V.16.C 45.60 to be passed at 2.25 P.M.
Arrive ST. OMER entraining point 6.50 P.M.

3. The Transport will be drawn up on road outside T.O's H.Q. with head of column just clear of ACQUIN - NORDAL road at 2.10 P.M. Riding horses will join the column at this point.

4. Route - ACQUIN - road junction V.16.C. 45.60 - Road junction V.16.d.2.5 - "NORDAL" - Road junction V.4.C.7.7 - BOISINGHEM - ZUDAUSQUES - LONGUEBORNE - ST MARTIN-AU-LAERT - X.35.C.5.0 Entraining point.
10 minutes halt will be called 10 minutes before each hour.

5. A lorry for Q.M. Stores will arrive at midday & will immediately be loaded. SGT. STEPHENS, 4/c BIRKETT & 4/c PIMM will accompany the lorry to entraining point.

6. An advance party consisting of 2/LT TEAGUE & 2 signallers (with 3 bicycles) will proceed with the train leaving at 6.50 P.M. today. They will report at ST OMER entraining point to O.C. 149. M.G. Coy for accommodation in the train. On arrival at MOREUIL they will report to Administrative Commandant VILLERS BRETONNEUX to take over Coy Billets at BLANGY TRONVILLE.

7. Rations & forage up to 10th inst will be taken.

8. Detraining Station MOREUIL.

9. Train will be loaded by the Company.
    (a) No. 4 Section will assist Transport personnel in loading animals.
    (b) No. 2 Section will load vehicles on to train.

Issued at 10 A.M.
10 Copies.

W.R. Thomson
Captain
O.C. 245 M.G. Coy.

SECRET.

OPERATION ORDER No 38. BY CAPTAIN. W.R. Thomson
COMMANDING 245 MACHINE GUN COY.

REFCE.
AMIENS. 17. 1/100.000.   10.3.18.

1. The Company will move by route march from BLANGY-TRONVILLE to VAUVILLERS tomorrow 11th March.

2. Parade 8.35 A.M. on road - head of column on GRANDE PLACE.
Pass starting point (railway crossing on road up to Main Road) at 9 A.M.

3. Route :- VILLERS-BRETONNEUX - MARCELCAVE - WIENCOURT - GUILLAUCOURT - HARBONNIÈRES - VAUVILLERS. about 15 miles.

4. Advance party: 2/LT LEE with 2 signallers will proceed to VAUVILLERS as advance billeting party - to arrive not later than 10 A.M.

5. A lorry will be available for moving A.M. Stores & blankets.
All blankets will be handed in at 8. A.M. to Stores.
Packs will be worn.

6. The Division is in G.H.Q Reserve & under 12 hours notice.

Reveille 6.30 A.M.
Breakfast 7 A.M.

Issued at 9 p.m.   W R Thomson Captain
10.3.18.   O.C. 245 M.G. Coy.

SECRET.   Copy No 1   13
                           App<u>x</u> 5

Warning Order No 39 by Capt. W. R. Thomson
         Commdg 245 M. G. Coy.

Ref<u>ce</u> AMIENS 17 1/100,000.   12<u>th</u> March 18.

1.   50<u>th</u> Div<u>n</u> is in A.H.Q. (FIFTH) & will be ready to move at 12 hours notice.
      The move may be carried out either by Strategical or by Tactical Trains.

2.   Entraining Station probably:

151<u>st</u> Bde. Group   VILLERS-BRETONNEUX.
      A move by Tactical Trains may be carried out at one entraining Station for the whole Division. This would probably be   GUILLAUCOURT.

3.   For purposes of entrainment 245 M.G. Coy. with 50<u>th</u> Batt<u>n</u> H.Q. will be in the 151<u>st</u> Inf. Bde. Group.

Issued at 8p.m.   W R Thomson Capt<u>n</u>
3 Copies   O.C. 245 M.G. Coy.

SECRET Copy No 14
App: 6.

Warning Order No 40 by Capt. W. R. Thomson
Commdg 245 M.G. Coy.

Ref: ST. QUENTIN 18 } 1/100,000
VALENCIENNES 12 }   13? March 18.

---

1. In the event of a hostile attack succeeding against certain portions of our line Brigades will be prepared to counter-attack as under

   149   in III Corps against BENAY & ESSIGNY
   150   in XIX "   "   LE VERGUIER & FERVEQUE F^m
   151   in VII "   "   RONSSOY, EPEHY, GOUZEAUCOURT

   245 M.G. Coy. will probably accompany the 151st Inf. Bde.

2. Movement will be carried out in Tactical Trains in accordance with Coy. W.O. No

3 Copies
Issued at 4 pm.

W R Thomson Capt.
O.C. 245 M.G. Coy.

Ref: Sheet 57C SE. 1/20,000.   App. 7   Copy No 1   15
                                  SECRET.

Tactical Instructions No 1
245 M. G. Coy.

1. The 50th Divn has been ordered to be prepared to counter-attack villages of METZ-EN-COUTURE assuming the enemy's line to run as indicated by the Brown Line. (Map No. 1.)

2. Right attack   150 Inf Bde.
   Left attack   151 do.
   Reserve   149 do.

3. Approach by night through EQUANCOURT to line W1a - V6b - P36c via valleys in V5a, W1c respectively.

4. Advance by night to line Q26c, Q25a.

5. 150, 151 & 245 M.G. Coys will cooperate as per Table "A" attached. 149 Coy will be in Reserve with 149 Bde in valley S. of DESSART WOOD.

6. 245 M.G. Coy HQ will be established with 151 Coy Group HQ in vicinity of 151 Bde H.Q.
   Batt: in vicinity of Divn H.Q - notified later.

7. Owing to the fact that battery positions are located on forward slopes all movement after dawn to be avoided.
   Emplacements & B/P slots will be dug during the night as time permits & concealed as far as possible.

8. A minimum of 40 Belt Boxes & 8 Boxes SAA per Battery will be carried up during the night.
   SAA dump will be arranged on road N. of FINS - location will be notified later.

9. Consolidating guns under Lt. DERBYSHIRE will be retained at Coy. H.Q. until definite information is forthcoming that the final objective is captured.

Batty	Unit	Location	Time	Task
C	245 M.G.Coy.	Q31a.40.75	(a) 0 to 0+15' (b) 0+25' to 0+49'	Q20c.7.7 to Q20c.0.9 Q14d.2.5 to Q14c.0.7
D	do.	Q31a.9.9	do.	do.
Consolidating Guns	do.	2 guns Q24b.3.4 2 guns Q19a.6.3	After capture of final objective	Fire N. along West Q20b. Fire N.E. Q13d. Q13c.

10. Lt. GRAVES assisted by 2/Lt. ATTWATER will be i/c the two Batteries supplied by Nos 2 & 3 Sect^ns - 8 guns. They will occupy the pos^ns selected during the reconnaissance on 19th inst.

11. Map showing all objectives, Div^l & Bd. Bdies, Battery pos^ns & ~~Consolidating~~ gun pos^ns is attached.

Issued at 6 p.m.
20.3.18.
6 Copies.

W R Thomson Capt.
O.C. 245 M.G. Coy.

TABLE "A."

Batty	Unit	Location	Time	Task
C	245 M G Coy.	Q31 a.40.75	(a) 0 to 0+15' (b) 0+25' to 0+49'	Q20 c.7.7 to Q20 c.0.9. Q14 d.2.5 to Q14 c.0.7.
D	do.	Q31 a.9.9.	do.	do.
Consolidating Guns	do.	2 guns Q24 b.3.4 2 guns Q19 a.6.3	After capture of final objective	Fire N. along line Q 20.D. Fire N.E. Q13 d. Q 13. c.

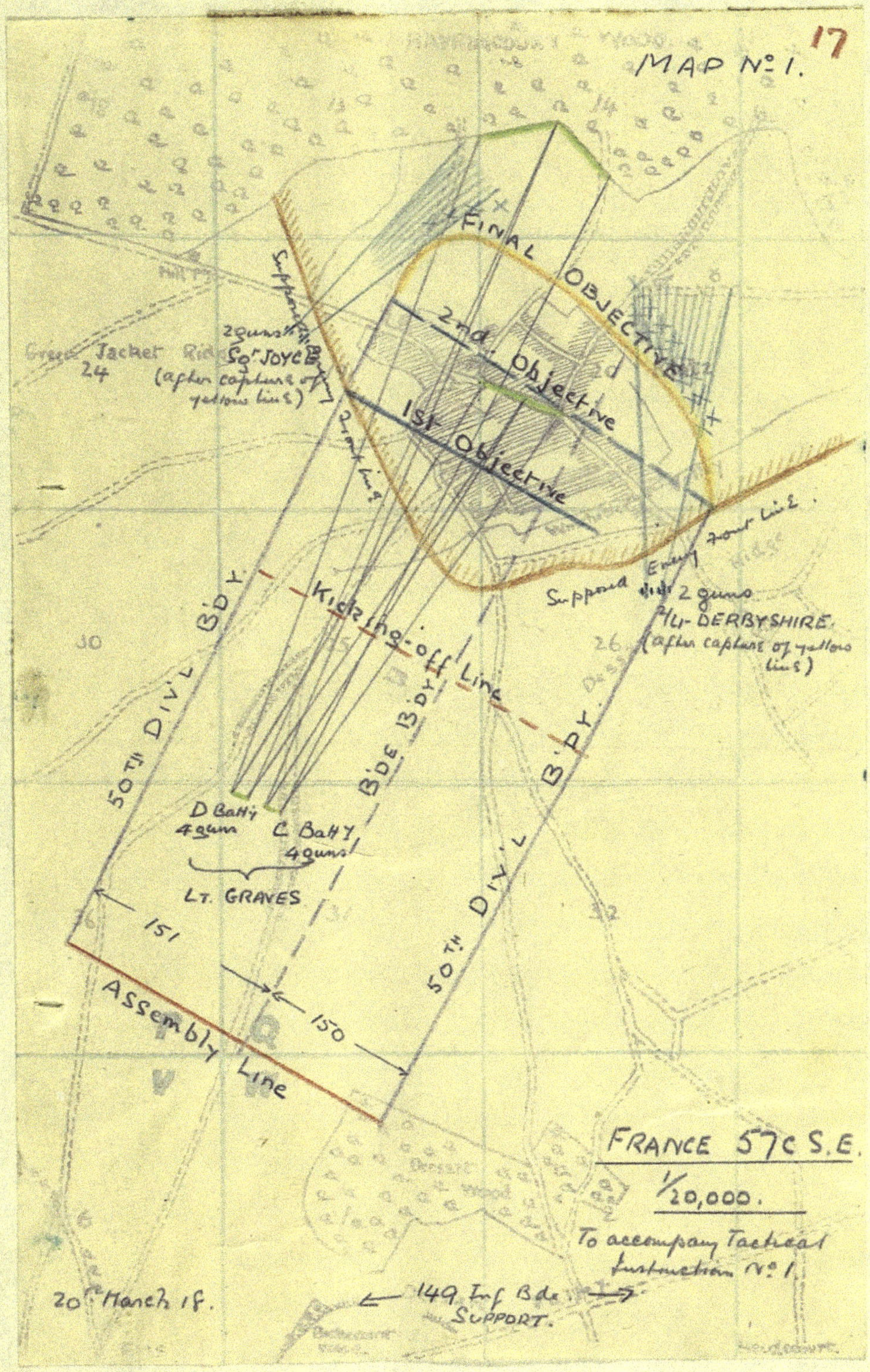
17
MAP No 1.
FINAL OBJECTIVE
2nd Objective
1st Objective
Kicking-off Line
Supposed Enemy front line
2 guns
4th DERBYSHIRE
(after capture of yellow line)
(after capture of yellow line)
Green Jacket Ridge
24
30
26
50th Div'l B'dy
B'de B'dy
D Batty
4 guns
C Batty
4 guns
Lt. GRAVES
151
150
Assembly Line
50th Div'l B'dy
FRANCE 57c S.E.
1/20,000.
To accompany Tactical Instruction No 1.
20th March 18.
149 Inf Bde
SUPPORT.

App x 8 18
Appendix 8.

Copies of Telegrams received from M.G. Battn:

1. All Coys. M 77 21 — AAA Coys will be prepared to move at 12 hours notice instead of 24 AAA In accordance with their respective Group Warning orders AAA Troops to remain in vicinity of Billets

   50th Battn M.G. Corps.
   6 A.M.   (Sd) HW Fletcher Lt.

2. All Coys. M.G. 82 21 — AAA Bde Groups will be ready to begin moving out of billets to entraining Stns. at 4 hours notice AAA Ack.

   50th Battn M.G. Corps.
   10 AM   (Sd) HW Fletcher Lt.

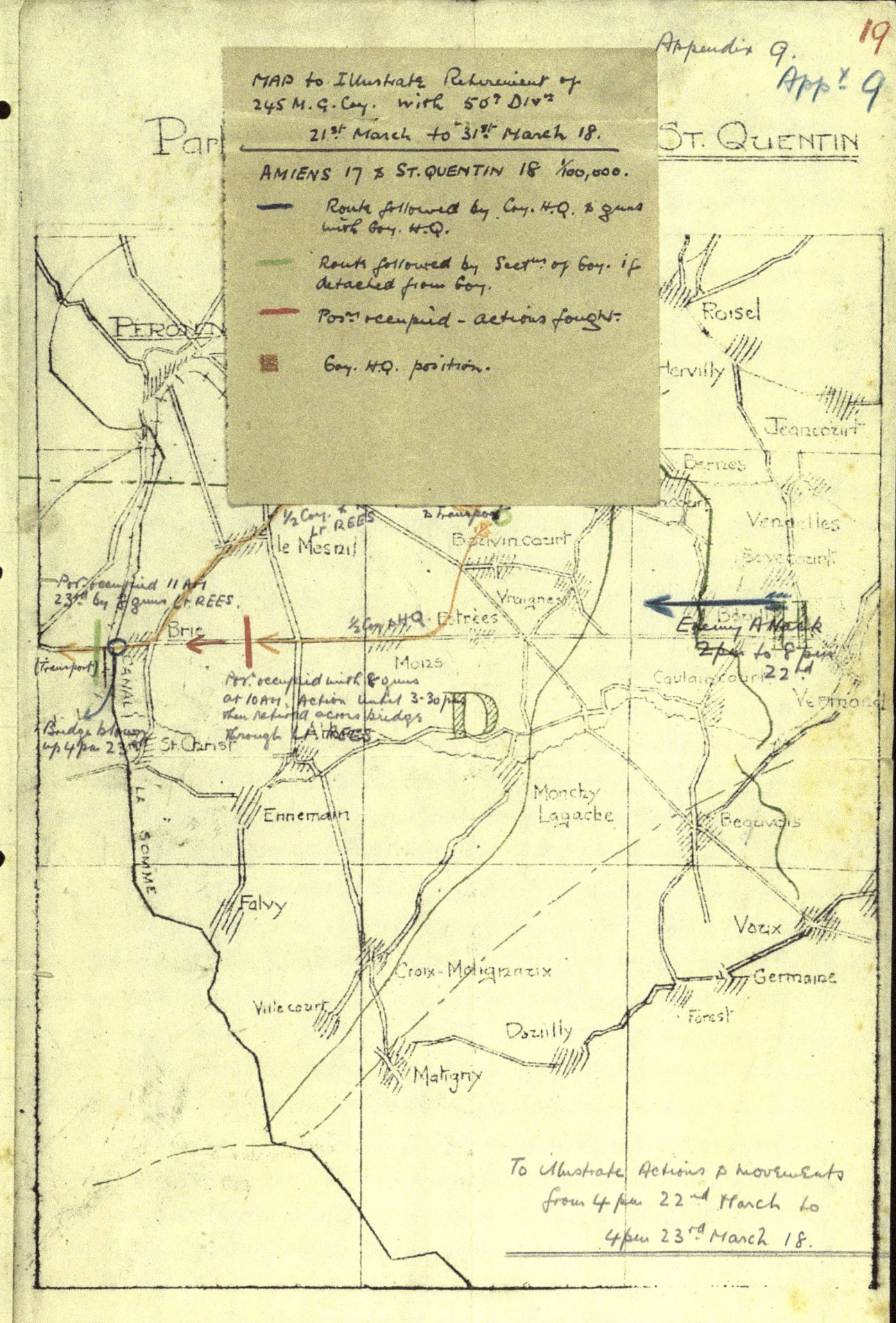

Appendix 9.
App 9
19

Parts of Sht. AMIENS & ST. QUENTIN

Scale 1:100,000

To illustrate Actions & movements
from 4 pm 22nd March to
4 pm 23rd March 18.

Issued 10 AM 22nd March 18.

W R Thomson Capt
O.C. 245 M.G. Coy.

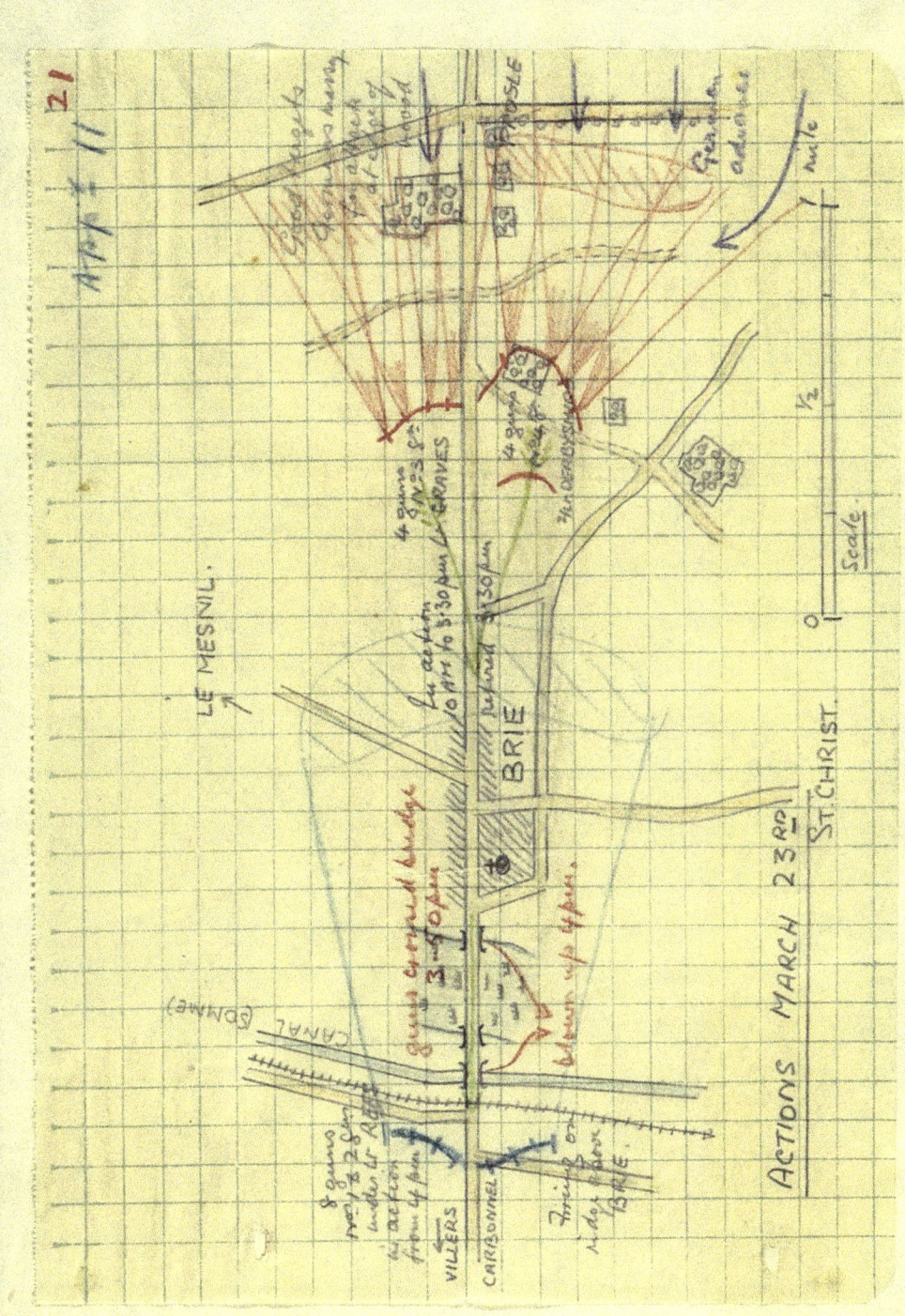

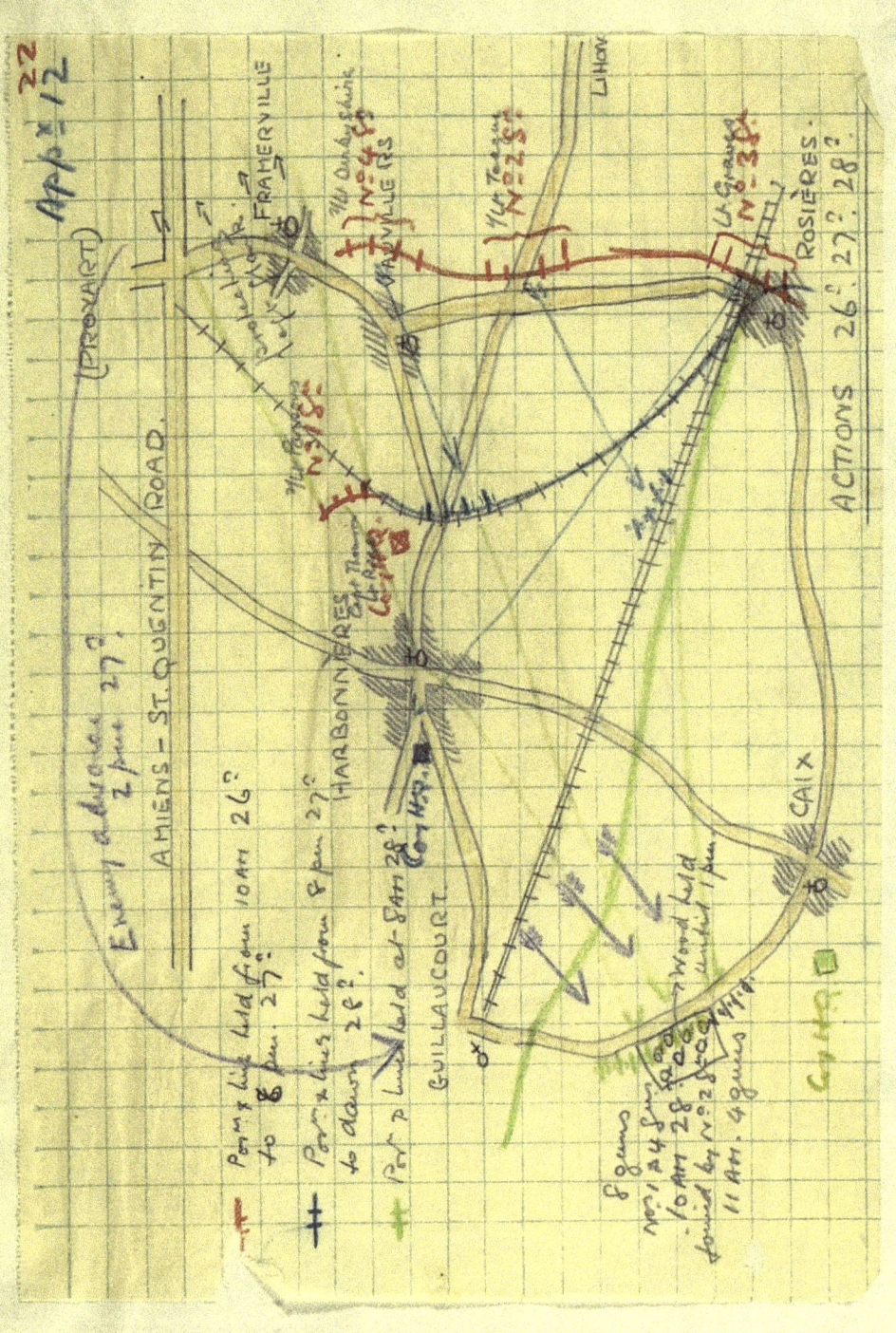

Copy No 1   App? 13   SECRET   23

Operation Order No 41 by Capt W R Thomson
Commdg 245 M.G. Coy.

Ref^{ce} AMIENS 1/100,000.   30th March 18.

___

1.   In accordance with 50th Divⁿ QX 8028 of 30th March all details with transport of Transport of 50th Divⁿ will Concentrate at once at SAINS-EN-AMIENOIS.

2.   245 M.G. Coy. will parade to move off at 9-30 A.M. Transport drawn up on road outside off^{rs} Mess.

3.   The Coy. will move by march route to SAINS-EN-AMIENOIS.

4.   A cyclist orderly will report to "Q" Office on arrival of the Coy. at SAINS.

Issued at 8-30 AM.   W R Thomson Captⁿ
3 Copies   O.C. 245 M.G. Coy.

App. 14   24

SECRET

XIX Corps Administrative Instructions No 98.
Ref. AMIENS 17 /100,000.   30 March 18.

1. Transport of Divs. will move in a N.W. direction. Transport surplus to immediate requirements being kept west of Transport required for the supply & ammunition of the fighting troops. Such surplus Transport to move forthwith remainder at discretion of Div. Commanders.

2. No transport will proceed W. of the LA CELLE RIVER except as stated in Para 3. Transport immediately required must be kept in close touch with fighting troops.

3. Roads are allotted as follows:—
   A. 1st Cavalry Div. Road Junct. at T of ST. ACREUIL to road junction 200 N. of A in FORET D'AHLY AMIENS
   B. 16th, 61st & 66th Divs. &C
   C. 2nd Cavalry Div. & 39th Div. &C.
   D. 18th 20th & 50th Divs. BOVES – SAINS-EN-AMIENOIS – RUMIGNY – HEBECOURT – VERS – CLAIRY.
   E. 3rd Cavalry Div. 24th & 30th Divn. &C.

4. All transport to be kept parked off the roads & concealed as far as possible from the East.

5. Personnel with transport will bivouac. All billets to be left clear for French Troops.

Issued at 11 A.M.   (Sd) A. T. G. MOIR
                                  Brigadier General
                         D.A.&Q.M.G.   XIX Corps

Forwarded by 50th Div.

App. 15   25

Copy No. 1   SECRET.

Coy. Warning Order No. 42 by Capt. W.R.Thomson
Comm'dg 245 M.G.Coy.
31st March '18

Ref: AMIENS 17 1/100,000.
    & ABBEVILLE 1/100,000.

1.   50th Div. (less Artillery) will start moving into the DAURIEZ Area today 31st March 1918 personnel by train. Transport by road.
     Entraining Station will be SALEUX.
     Further orders will be issued later.

2.   Transport will move by road staging twice. Night 31/1st April at BOURDON & night 1/2nd April at DOMVAST.

3.   150th Bde. Group will move off at 11.35 AM.

4.   For this move 245 M.G. Coy. will be in the 150th Bde Group. Lt. SEARANCKE will work with Lt. Wood & 2/Lt. TOMLINSON of Bn. H.Q. & 150 MG Coys Transport respectively.

5.   The Coy. will prepare to move by road to SALEUX this afternoon.

Issued at 8 AM.   W.R.Thomson Capt.
4 Copies.   OC 245 M.G.Coy.

www.ingramcontent.com/pod-product-compliance
Lightning Source LLC
Chambersburg PA
CBHW081410160426
43193CB00013B/2149